THE PROPHECIES OF
THE BRAHAN SEER

Coinneach Odhar Fiosaiche

ALEXANDER MACKENZIE

With a Foreword, Commentary
and Conclusion by

ELIZABETH SUTHERLAND

CONSTABLE   LONDON

First edition May 1877 Inverness
Second edition February 1878 Inverness
Revised edition 1899
Subsequent editions 1903, 1907, 1925
Reissued July 1970
Second impression January 1972
This edition first published in Great Britain 1977
by Constable and Company Limited
3 The Lanchesters, 162 Fulham Palace Road
London W6 9ER
Foreword, Commentary and Conclusion
Copyright © 1977 by Elizabeth Sutherland
Reprinted thirteen times
Paperback edition 1998
Reprinted 1999, 2001
ISBN 0 09 478460 4

Printed in Great Britain by
St Edmundsbury Press Limited
Bury St Edmunds, Suffolk

A CIP catalogue record for this book
is available from the British Library

Contents

Foreword to 1977 Edition, by Elizabeth Sutherland   11

Dedication to First Edition, by Alexander Mackenzie, 1877   17

Preface to 1878 Edition, by Alexander Mackenzie   19

Foreword to 1899 Edition, by Andrew Lang   21

The Prophecies of the Brahan Seer   25

Prophecies which Might be Attributed to Natural Shrewdness   35

Unfulfilled Prophecies   40

Prophecies as to the Fulfilment of which there is a Doubt   58

Prophecies Wholly or Partly Fulfilled   62

Sketch of the Family of Seaforth   104

Seaforth's Dream   110

Seaforth's Doom   112

The Seer's Death   119

The Fulfilment of the Seaforth Prophecy   124

'Lament for the Last of the Seaforths' by Sir Walter Scott   133

Conclusion: Who Was Coinneach Odhar? by Elizabeth
     Sutherland   135

Bibliography   149

Index   151

The Commentary in each chapter, set in smaller type, is by Elizabeth Sutherland

Illustrations

between pages 64 and 65

Uig Sands, Lewis (*Aerofilms Ltd*)

Port of Ness, Lewis (*Aerofilms Ltd*)

Dunvegan Castle, Isle of Skye (*Scottish Tourist Board*)

The Five Sisters of Kintail from Ratagan (*W. J. Webster*)

Hugh Miller of Cromarty (*Scottish National Portrait Gallery*)

Tomnahurich, Inverness (*W. J. Webster*)

The Caledonian Canal at Muirton, Inverness (*W. J. Webster*)

The old Leanach Cottage, Culloden (*W. J. Webster*)

The Pump Room, Strathpeffer (*W. J. Webster*)

The Eagle Stone, Strathpeffer (*W. J. Webster*)

Fairburn Tower, near Muir of Ord (*W. J. Webster*)

Kilcoy Castle (*Castle Studio, Inverness*)

Redcastle (*W. J. Webster*)

between pages 96 and 97

Avoch (*W. J. Webster*)

Foulis Castle (*Captain Patrick Munro of Foulis*)

Balnagown Castle (*W. J. Webster*)

Brahan Castle (*W. J. Webster*)

Isabella, wife of Kenneth, third Earl of Seaforth
  (*Ross and Cromarty District Council*)

7

Illustrations

Kenneth, third Earl of Seaforth
  (*Ross and Cromarty District Council*)

Francis Humberston Mackenzie (*W. J. Webster*)

Fortrose Cathedral (*W. J. Webster*)

Memorial Tablet, Fortrose Cathedral (*W. J. Webster*)

The Hood Memorial (*W. J. Webster*)

Commemorative Stone, Chanonry Point, Fortrose
  (*W. J. Webster*)

Acknowledgements

I would like to thank the following, for their help and advice:

Hugh Barron, Inverness. The Earl of Cromartie, Castle Leod, Strathpeffer. Joe Fisher, ALA, Local History Librarian, Mitchell Library, Glasgow. The late Rev John Macinnes, MA, PH D, DD, of Fortrose. John Maclennan, journalist, Culbokie. Andrew Matheson of Brahan. The Rev William Matheson, MA, of the Department of Celtic Studies, Edinburgh University. Captain Patrick Munro of Foulis. R. W. Munro and the Clan Munro Association. Francis Thompson, author, Inverness and Stornoway. W. J. Webster, photographer, Inverness. Ian C. Young, Ipswich.

E.S.

Foreword

by Elizabeth Sutherland

Coinneach Odhar, generally known as the Brahan Seer, is a name as familiar to the Highlanders of Scotland as the Prophet Isaiah. Over the centuries his predictions have been as well known and reverently repeated as Bible tales, yet the man behind the Seer is as mysterious and elusive as his prophecies are awe-inspiring and portentous.

Most of what we know about the Brahan Seer derives from the oral tradition of the Gael. The long stormy nights of a northern winter were not necessarily occasions of dread to the Highlander in days gone by. Folk would gather together in the Ceilidh house, a cottage divided into three rooms with one door in the byre which led into the kitchen, and the sleeping apartment beyond. In the centre of the kitchen a slightly raised pavement held the peat fire, whose smoke found its way to a hole in the turfed roof. As neighbours gathered and the company grew, so the circle round the fire expanded to let all warm themselves. The man of the house, elderly, possibly a church officer, certainly a bard or musician, welcomed all, and everyone was expected to contribute to the entertainment. A large oak chair was placed in a particular spot 'where the sun rose', and its occupant was expected to start the proceedings. Out of natural modesty rather than inability, it was usually last to be occupied.

The women's fingers flew over their knitting and the younger members were expected to take a turn at working the nets in the shadowy corners, while the ancient folklore of the country, the poetry and music, the proverbs and predictions were repeated from one generation to another down the centuries.

Nothing was written down. Poetry was learned by rote and passed from one generation of bards to the next; stories were learned by

11

repetition at the Ceilidh hearth; and because folklore was a living art, the old tales were gradually altered and embellished according to the credulity of the listener and the imaginative powers of the reciter.

Thus we owe a debt of gratitude to Alexander Mackenzie who, with the help of Mr Donald Macintyre, a schoolmaster of Arpafeelie in the Black Isle, and Mr A. B. Maclennan, author of *The Petty Seer*, collected and wrote down as many tales and prophecies connected with Coinneach Odhar as he could find. These he later published as a series of articles in the *Celtic Magazine*, edited by himself in Inverness.

The first collected edition of the *Prophecies of the Brahan Seer*, printed in May 1877 as a shorter reprint from the *Celtic Magazine*, was sold out in a few months. The second edition, considerably enlarged, was subscribed extensively in advance and was dedicated to the Rev Alexander McGregor, MA, of the West Church, Inverness, who contributed to a lengthy appendix on the 'Superstitions of the Highlanders'. A revised edition, published by Aeneas Mackay of Stirling and edited by Andrew Lang, appeared in 1899, the year of Mackenzie's death. Thereafter, these and three further editions (1903, 1907 and 1925) were to become collectors' items, with never less than fifty readers on the waiting list at Inverness Public Library, until it was reprinted by the Sutherland Press, Golspie, in 1970.

Alexander Mackenzie, known as the 'Clach' after the name of his first shop in Inverness called 'Clachnacuddin House', was one of the best-known Highlanders of his day, notable as politician, editor and clan historian.

Born on a croft in Gairloch in 1838, he had little opportunity for schooling and at an early age earned his living as navvy, ploughman and labourer. About 1860 he joined the Scotch Drapery Trade in England, and soon made his way as a businessman. In 1869 he settled in Inverness, first as a clothier, then as editor and publisher of the *Celtic Magazine*, which ran from 1875 to 1888, and the *Scottish Highlander*, 1885 to 1898. He published several clan histories, including that of the Mackenzies, all works of genealogical value, and was a founder member of the Inverness Gaelic Society.

According to Mackenzie, the Brahan Seer was a man called Kenneth Mackenzie, commonly known as Coinneach Odhar – dun-coloured Kenneth – who was born on Mackenzie land in Baile-na-Cille in Uig on the Isle of Lewis, and who came to live near Loch Ussie and work as a labourer on the Brahan estate, seat of the Seaforth Mackenzies, some time between 1660 and 1675.

Apart from Alexander Mackenzie's sources, there are, however, other references to Coinneach Odhar which place him a century earlier, prophesying in Skye, and two historical references in which he is accused of witchcraft in 1577/1578. It would appear that these references, quoted fully in the Conclusion, cannot reasonably be attributed to the same man; yet such was the power of his name and the awe surrounding his alleged gifts of prediction, that he has continued to challenge the curiosity of generation upon generation of Highlanders.

His prophecies are widely distributed throughout Ross and Cromarty and are largely concerned with the Mackenzie clan, in particular with the Seaforth Mackenzies. After a quarrel with Isabella, wife of the third Earl of Seaforth, he predicted the doom of her race which was to come true with uncanny accuracy after the death of the seventh Earl in 1783, when the earldom became extinct. The Seaforth line, as predicted, then changed and reverted to a direct descendant of Isabella through her third son, in the person of Francis Humberston Mackenzie, who was in 1797 to be created a British peer as Baron Seaforth and Baron Mackenzie of Kintail.

There are several versions all given in the book of how Coinneach Odhar came by his divining stone. This was said to be round with a hole in it like a spindle whorl through which he 'saw' his visions. Most versions agree that the stone was necessary to him in making his predictions and that the eye he used was *cam* or blind to normal vision.

Paradoxically, the climate of opinion, scientific and lay, is a good deal kinder towards the paranormal today than it was a hundred years ago when Mackenzie first began to collect the prophecies of Coinneach Odhar. Somewhat shamefacedly he writes: 'Not so much with the view of protecting ourselves from the charge of a belief in such superstitious folly (for we hesitate to acknowledge any such belief) but as a slight palliative for obtruding such nonsense on the public . . .' Andrew Lang, in his foreword to the 1899 edition of the Prophecies, is less coy, but rightly insists that predictions should be taken down before fulfilment. 'Unless this is done, the predictions as matters of evidence go for nothing.'

There are three Gaelic names to describe the faculty. These are *Da Radharc, Da Shealladh* and *Taibhs Searachd*; and of these *Da*

Shealladh is in most common usage. Literally it means two sights, the vision of this world, ordinarily possessed by all, and the 'dream vision', the third eye which enables some to see apparitions of the dead or living. The object seen is called in Gaelic *taibhs* and the seer *taibhsear*. The *taibhs* is entirely independent of the person it represents, nor is it encouraged or cultivated by the *taibhsear*. To distinguish between a true *taibhs* and a flaw in the seer's eyesight or digestion, the *taibhsear* would sometimes stoop and stand quickly. If the vision did not disappear, he knew it was a true *taibhs*.

The gift of second sight was not considered enviable or desirable. Sometimes it ran in families which suggests that it was a faculty capable of being inherited like a talent for music, but equally it was capable of being possessed by anyone and to differing degrees. Sometimes it appeared in early life, sometimes in old age. Nor was it voluntary. Vision came without choice and was deemed an affliction rather than a privilege.

It is possible that second sight originated in a late Stone Age priest-hood associated with ancestor worship. Its purpose was to keep in touch with the spirits who inhabited the burial mounds who were later to be confused with the *sithean* which translates as fairy-folk. The Rev Robert Kirk in 1690/1 wrote an entertaining treatise on the *sithean* entitled *The Secret Common-Wealth* about 'the nature and actions of the Subterranean (and for the most part) Invisible People heirtofor going under the name of Elves, Faunes, and Fairies, or the like . . . as they are described by those who have the Second Sight'. In it he describes several ways in which second sight could be obtained. For example it could be a direct gift from the fairies in order to communicate some important event. Or it could be received at conception by a seventh son through some virtue in the mother's womb which reached a peak with the seventh child and thereafter declined. Kirk himself was a seventh son.

Women, according to Kirk did not make good seers. It was not that they did not have visions but rather that they were incapable of correct interpretation.

According to Martin in his *Description of the Western Isles of Scotland*, at the sight of the vision 'the eyelids of the person are erected and the eyes continue staring until the object vanishes. There was one seer in Skye whose eyelids turned up so far inwards that he had to draw them down with his fingers or get others to do so.'

Foreword

One of the most interesting books to be written on the subject appeared in 1773, entitled *A Treatise on the Second Sight* by Theophilus Insulanus, who was thought to have been a minister called Macpherson who travelled widely in the Western isles. In his book he deals with what he calls 'the undoubted fact of second sight', and gives many authenticated instances.

Boswell, in his *Journal of a Tour in the Hebrides with Samuel Johnson LL.D* gave several instances and later Dr Johnson was to give his own wonderfully succinct definition:

'The Second Sight is an impression made either by the mind upon the eye or the eye upon the mind, by which things distant or future are perceived and seen as if they were present.'

During the nineteenth century, at a time when the Highlands were undergoing a religious revival, second sight was to take on a slightly different aspect, not exactly in the line of direct inspiration of prophecy, yet containing a strongly religious flavour. Perhaps the earliest exponent of this was the Rev John Morrison, more commonly called the Petty Seer, some of whose authenticated predictions have been ascribed to the Brahan Seer, and whose works were collected by A. B. Maclennan, one of Alexander Mackenzie's sources.

Dr John Kennedy, in his book *The Days of the Fathers in Ross-shire*, published in 1861, which deals with religious life in the Highlands during his youth, writes at length about 'the Men' who had this particular gift of vision. 'The Men' were so called to distinguish them from ministers, some of whom were similarly gifted. Dr Kennedy states that this was a gift vouchsafed to particularly pious people direct from the Holy Spirit, and was not to be confused with the Old Testament idea of prophecy. One of many examples of this sort of second sight concerned a Mr Mackay of Hope in the Black Isle, who because of ill-health was unable to attend church to hear a well-known preacher. When the family returned to tell him about the wonderful sermon they had heard, he was able to quote it to them, text, message and exhortation.

Since the days of 'the Men' and those earlier seers who were credited with the gift, the perception of second sight has changed. It has become confused with folklore tales of ghosts in shrouds, disembodied daggers, phantom funerals and the like. But the desire to know the future is still as strong in mankind as ever it was. The seer's place has been taken by the psychic, the astrologist and the tarot card reader, some of whose methods and motives would be abhorrent to the true *taibhsear*.

However this Foreword is not meant to question the existence of pre-cognition as exemplified by the Highland gift of second sight. As Francis Thompson, one of the Highlands' leading historians of today, writes: 'My own attitude is that it is an indisputable part of the human mind's ability. Some people are possessed of the gift, mainly I suspect because their forebears had it and were able to pass it on through their ability to exercise that part of the mind or brain concerned with "the third eye". For most of us the ability has atrophied through lack of use.'

Nor are this Foreword and the Conclusion concerned to debunk Coinneach Odhar. Far from it. Research by such eminent scholars as the Rev William Matheson recently of the Department of Celtic Studies at Edinburgh University has established the existence of him as a historical fact. Further research may reveal more.

The true value of Alexander Mackenzie's book does not lie so much in the fact that it is a historical account of the life and sayings of one man, but that herein may be found a unique collection of old Highland lore which was fast vanishing a hundred years ago when he first published the results of his painstaking research. It also gives us a glimpse into the way that fact may be woven into fantasy, truth into myth, over the passing years in the oral tradition.

More important, it details the prophecies themselves, a valuable collection of utterances whoever their author, which will continue to cause wonder and speculation in future generations as they have done in the past.

E.S.
October 1976

Dedication to First Edition

Preface to the 1878 Edition

The First Edition of the *Prophecies of the Brahan Seer*, which appeared only eight months ago, went out of print in a few months; and though only a reprint from the *Celtic Magazine*, without even a re-setting of the types, and containing many blemishes of style and arrangement, it was received by the Press and the public in a manner for which I am glad so soon to have this agreeable opportunity of expressing my gratitude. This Edition is considerably enlarged; and I venture to hope it will be found in all respects superior to the first. I acknowledge with pleasure the fact that the public and the trade have already accepted it, to a great extent on trust, by subscribing for it extensively in advance. No doubt this is largely due to the confidence placed, by a large number of such as take an interest in Celtic matters, in my friend the Rev ALEXANDER M'GREGOR, MA, who has written the main part of the APPENDIX on the 'Superstition of the Highlanders', published herewith, specially for this Edition – a small portion only being a re-cast of his articles on the same subject which recently appeared in the *Celtic Magazine*.

A.M.
Celtic Magazine Office
Inverness, 9th February 1878

Foreword to the 1899 Edition

by Andrew Lang

Mr Mackay has asked me to make a few comments on Mr Mackenzie's *Prophecies of the Brahan Seer*, and I do so for the sake of old times and old ideas. Unlike Mr Mackenzie, I can unblushingly confess the belief that there probably are occasional instances of second sight, that is, of 'premonitions'. I know too many examples among persons of my acquaintance, mostly Lowlanders and English, to have any doubt about the matter. Hegel was of the same opinion, and was not ashamed to include second sight in his vast philosophic system.* As to the *modus* of second sight, 'how it is done', in fact, I have no theory. If there is a physical element in man, if there is something more than a mechanical result of physical processes in nerve, brain and blood, then we cannot set any limit to the range of 'knowledge supernormally acquired'. 'Time and space are only hallucinations,' as a philosopher has audaciously remarked. They may be transcended by the spirit in man, *et voila pourquoi votre fille est muette!* This explanation, of course, is of the vaguest, but I have no better to suggest.

By an odd coincidence, two cases of second sight, of recent date, in the experience of an educated lady, reached me yesterday at first hand, and, as I pen these words, another (knowledge of death at a distance) comes to me from a distinguished philologist. But he thinks he was ten minutes out in his reckoning, which, allowing for differences of watches, is not much. A fourth case is from a Royal Academician, an intimate friend. He and a lady,

Philosophie der Gheistes, werke vii. 179. Berlin, 1845.

also of my acquaintance, were being shown over a beautiful new house by the owner. My friend, in the owner's bedroom, turned pale. The lady, when they went out, asked him what ailed him. 'I saw X——' (the owner of the house) 'lying dead in his bed.' X—— died within a month, which would be thought fair work in the Highlands.

An odder case occurred last year. On June 15, a lady, well known to me, and in various fields of literature, told me that, calling on another lady the day before, she had seen a vision of a man, previously unknown to her, who thrust a knife into her friend's left side. I offered to bet £100 against fulfilment. In autumn my friend, again calling at the same house, met the man of her vision on the doorsteps. Entering, she found her friend dying, as her constitution did not rally after an operation on her left side, performed by the man of vision, who was a surgeon. This is much in the Highland manner. Of the Seers here alluded to (and I might add many other modern instances in my own knowledge), only one was Celtic. For savage examples which illustrate the belief (though evidence cannot, of course, be procured with exactness), I may be permitted to refer to my *Making of Religion* (pp 72–158). The kind of story is always the same. And the legends of St Columba, in Adamnan, are much on a par, in many cases, with modern examples in *The Proceedings of the Society for Psychical Research*. The uniformity of the reports argues the existence of some facts at their base.

While I am credulous to this extent, I vastly prefer modern cases, at first hand, and corroborated (as when I can swear that the lady told me of her vision before its fulfilment), to the rumours of the Brahan Seer. We can scarcely ever, except as to the deaf Seaforth, find any evidence that the prophecies were recorded before the event. In many cases fulfilment could only occur, either in the ancient fighting Clan society, or under its revival, to which we cannot look with much confidence. The prophecies about sheep one has no evidence to prove earlier than, say, 1770. As to the burning of the Seer, if it really had clerical sanction, why are Kirk Sessions' Registers not brought forward as proof?

Have they been examined for this purpose? We are, in fact, dealing with poetic legend, not with evidence.

In one respect Kenneth is peculiar, among Highland Seers. He is a 'Crystal-gazer', whether his 'gibber' (as Australian savages call divining stones) was blue, or grey, or pearly, perforated or not. This use of stones, usually crystals, or black stones, I have found among Australians, Tonkaways, Aztecs, Incas, Samoyeds, Polynesians, Maoris, Greeks, Egyptians, in Fez: water, ink or blood being also employed to stare at. The whole topic is discussed in my book already cited, with many modern examples. Now I do not, elsewhere, know more than one or two cases of this kind of divination in the Highlands. The visions are usually spontaneous and uninvoked, except when the seer uses the blade-bone of a sheep. In the interests of Folk Lore, or Psychology, or both, people who have the opportunity should record cases of the use of divining stones in the Highlands. It is even more desirable that the statements of second-sighted men (they are common enough, to my personal knowledge, in Sutherland, Lochaber and Glencoe) *should be taken down before fulfilment.* Unless this is done, the predictions, as matter of evidence, go for nothing. We must try to discover the percentage of failures before we can say whether the successes are not due to chance, coincidence, or to mis-statement, or to mere imposture. I have little or no doubt that the Ferrintosh story (told in this book) is a misconception, based on the actual calamity at Fearn, long after the Seer was dead. In fact, like Dr Johnson, I want more evidence. He was ready to believe, but unconvinced. I am rather more credulous, but it would be very easy to upset my faith, and certainly it cannot be buttressed by vague reports on the authority of tradition. It may be urged that to inquire seriously into such things is to encourage superstition. But if inquiry merely unearthed failure and imposture, even superstition would be discouraged.

The Prophecies of the Brahan Seer

Coinneach Odhar Fiosaiche

The gift of prophecy, second sight, or *Taibh-searachd*, claimed for and believed by many to have been possessed, in an eminent degree, by Coinneach Odhar, the Brahan Seer, is one, the belief in which scientific men and others of the present day accept as unmistakable signs of looming, if not of actual insanity. We all are, or would be considered, scientific in these days. It will, therefore, scarcely be deemed prudent for anyone who wishes to lay claim to the slightest modicum of common sense, to say nothing of an acquaintance with the elementary principles of science, to commit to paper his ideas on such a subject, unless he is prepared, in doing so, to follow the common horde in their all but universal scepticism.

Without committing ourselves to any specific faith on the subject, however difficult it may be to explain away what follows on strictly scientific grounds, we shall place before the reader the extraordinary predictions of the Brahan Seer. We have had slight experiences of our own, which we would hesitate to dignify by the name of second sight. It is not, however, with our own experiences that we have at present to do, but with the 'Prophecies' of Coinneach Odhar Fiosaiche.

As we have seen in the Foreword, there are several Gaelic terms for those gifted with the second sight. *Fiosaiche* is not one of them. This translates literally as 'the one who knows' in the occult sense and is synonomous today with 'sorcerer'.

He is beyond comparison the most distinguished of all our High-land seers, and his prophecies have been known throughout the whole country for more than two centuries. The popular faith in them has been, and still continues to be, strong and widespread. Sir Walter Scott, Sir Humphrey Davy, Mr Morrit, Lockhart and other eminent contemporaries of the 'Last of the Seaforths' firmly believed in them. Many of them were well known, and recited from generation to generation, centuries before they were fulfilled. Some of them have been fulfilled in our own day, and many are still unfulfilled.

Not so much with the view of protecting ourselves from the charge of a belief in such superstitious folly (for we would hesitate to acknowledge any such belief), but as a slight palliation for ob-truding such nonsense on the public, we may point out, by the way, that the sacred writers – who are now believed by many of the would-be-considered-wise to have been behind the age, and not near so wise and far-seeing as we are – believed in second sight, witchcraft and other visions of a supernatural kind. But then we shall be told by our scientific friends that the Bible itself is becom-ing obsolete, and that it has already served its turn; being only suited for an unenlightened age in which men like Shakespeare, Milton, Newton, Bacon and such unscientific men could be con-sidered distinguished. The truth is that on more important topics than the one we are now considering, the Bible is laid aside by many of our would-be scientific lights, whenever it treats of any-thing beyond the puny comprehension of the minds and intellec-tual vision of these omniscient gentlemen. We have all grown so scientific that the mere idea of supposing anything possible which is beyond the intellectual grasp of the scientific enquirer cannot be entertained, although even he must admit, that in many cases, the greatest men in science, and the mightiest intellects, find it impossible to understand or explain away many things as to the existence of which they have no possible doubt. We even find the clergy slightly inconsistent in questions of this kind. They solemnly desire to impress us with the fact that ministering spirits hover about the couches and apartments in which the dying Christian is drawing near to the close of his existence, and preparing to throw off his mortal coil; but were we to suggest the possibility of any mere human being, in any conceivable manner, having had indications of the presence of these ghostly visitors, or discovering any signs or premonitions of the early departure of a relative or of an intimate friend, our heathen ideas and devious wanderings from the safe channel of clerical orthodoxy and consistent inconsistency, would be howled against, and paraded before the faithful as the grossest superstition, with an enthusiasm and relish possible only to a straight-laced ecclesiastic. Clerical inconsistency is, however, not our present theme.

Many able men have written on the second sight, and to some of them we shall refer in the following pages; meanwhile our purpose is to place before the reader the Prophecies of the Brahan Seer, as far as we have been able to procure them. We are informed that a considerable collection of them has been made by the late Alexander Cameron of Lochmaddy, author of the *History and Traditions of the Isle of Skye*, but we were unable to discover into whose possession the manuscript found its way; we hope, however, that this reference may bring it to light.

Kenneth Mackenzie, better known as Coinneach Odhar, the Brahan Seer (according to Mr Maclennan), was born at Baile-na-Cille, in the Parish of Uig and Island of Lews, about the beginning of the seventeenth century. Nothing particular is recorded of his early life, but when he had just entered his teens, he received a stone in the following manner, by which he could reveal the future destiny of man: – While his mother was tending her cattle in a summer shealing on the side of a ridge called Cnoceothail, which overlooks the burying-ground of Baile-na-Cille, in Uig, she saw, about the still hour of midnight, the whole of the graves in the churchyard opening, and a vast multitude of people of every age, from the newly-born babe to the grey-haired sage, rising from their graves, and going away in every conceivable direction. In about an hour they began to return, and were all soon after back in their graves, which closed upon them as before. But, on scanning the burying-place more closely, Kenneth's mother observed one grave, near the side, still open. Being a courageous woman, she determined to ascertain the cause of this singular circumstance, so, hastening to the grave, and placing her *cuigeal* (distaff) athwart its mouth (for she had heard it said that the spirit could not enter the grave again while that instrument was upon it), she watched the result. She had not to wait long, for in a minute or two she noticed a fair lady coming in the direction of the churchyard, rushing through the air, from the north. On her arrival, the fair one addressed her thus – 'Lift thy distaff from off my grave, and let me enter my dwelling of the dead.' 'I shall do so,' answered the other, 'when you explain to me what detained you so long after your neighbours.' 'That you shall soon hear,' the ghost replied; 'My journey was much longer than theirs – I had to go all the way to Norway.' She then addressed her: – 'I am a daughter of the King of Norway; I was drowned while bathing in that country; my body was found on the beach close to where you now stand, and I was interred in this grave. In remembrance of me, and as a small reward for your intrepidity and courage, I shall possess you of a valuable secret – go and find in yonder lake a small round blue stone, which give to your son, Kenneth, who by it shall reveal future events.' She did as requested, found the stone, and gave it to her son, Kenneth.

This legend, which owes its origin to Norse mythology, is quoted in much the same form in the Bannatyne History of the Macleods, thought to have been written by Sir William Macleod Bannatyne of Kames, who died in 1838. According to him, Coinneach Odhar was the most famour seer in the Highlands, whose prophecies foretell of chiefs and clans, of tribes and families, of kingdoms and royal dynasties, and which are, says the Rev Canon R. C. Macleod of Macleod who edited the Manuscript, 'nothing more than prophetic history'.

The Manuscript places him as a contemporary of Tormod Macleod, the last Dunvegan chief who could not write, and who died in 1585. His mother received the 'small, black and beautiful pebble' from the ghost of the Northland princess, who said, 'Give this to the child who will be born to you, when he is seven years old.'

On Kenneth's seventh birthday his mother, who had forgotten the ghost's admonition, told the lad to call his father who was at work in the field. When Kenneth refused, she remembered the pebble and gave it to him in exchange for his obedience. When he took it he 'saw' a large whale stranded in a nearby cave.

One of his prophecies quoted in the Manuscript stated that 'When the Gael begins to wear the garb of the stranger, a dark-haired man in white hose and a green plaid will cross and recross the Sound of Scarpa, a thing which has never been done and never will be done but this once.'

This happened in 1784 at the time when the Disarming Act forbade the wearing of Highland dress. Phillip Macdonald, dressed as foretold, did cross and recross the Sound on a Sunday in August when the tide was low, 'for a frolic'. A hundred people saw it happen.

When he was about fifty, Coinneach prophesied the downfall of the Macleods. The Chief's men ambushed him and tried to take away his pebble, but he flung it into a nearby loch, preferring to see it lost than fall into other hands. According to the Manuscript, his grave can still be seen at Ness.

Another Norse tale told in Lewis describes how Coinneach Odhar found his stone in a raven's nest, and how anyone may acquire the gift of prophecy. First find a raven's nest. Take the eggs home, boil them and when cool return them to the nest. The raven will then try to hatch them. When nothing happens, she will fly off in search of the Victory Stone. When she has found it, she will put it in the nest with the eggs to encourage their hatching. When the raven next leaves the nest, take the stone. This charm will assure victory in battle and endow the finder with the gift of prophecy.

It is interesting to compare the Norse and Highland superstitions regarding the raven, which features in many of Coinneach Odhar's prophecies. In Norse mythology, the 'Bird of Odin' was regarded with respect, as it was able to prophesy victory or defeat in battle and act as guide to the Valkyries. To the Highlander it was a bird of ill-omen and a harbinger of death. The old Gaelic curse, 'a raven's death to you', comes from the belief that the birds would kill their parents on Easter Day.

No sooner had he thus received the gift of divination than his fame spread far and wide. He was sought after by the gentry throughout the length and breadth of the land, and no special assembly of theirs was complete unless Coinneach Odhar was amongst them. Being born on the lands of Seaforth, in the Lews, he was more associated with that family than with any other in the country, and he latterly removed to the neighbourhood of Loch Ussie, on the Brahan estate, where he worked as a common labourer on a neighbouring farm. He was very shrewd and clear-headed, for one in his menial position; was always ready with a smart answer, and if any attempted to raise the laugh at his expense, seldom or ever did he fail to turn it against his tormentors.

There are various other versions of the manner in which he became possessed of the power of divination. According to one – His mistress, the farmer's wife, was unusually exacting with him, and he, in return, continually teased, and, on many occasions, expended much of his natural wit upon her, much to her annoyance and chagrin. Latterly, his conduct became so unbearable that she decided upon disposing of him in a manner which would save her any future annoyance. On one occasion, his master having sent him away to cut peats, which in those days were, as they now are in more remote districts, the common article of fuel, it was necessary to send him his dinner, he being too far from the house to come home to his meals, and the farmer's wife so far carried out her intention of destroying him, that she poisoned his dinner. It was somewhat late in arriving, and the future prophet feeling exhausted from his honest exertions in his master's interest and from want of food, lay down on the heath and fell into a heavy slumber. In this position he was suddenly awakened by feeling something cold in his breast, which on examination he found to be a small white stone, with a hole through the centre. He looked through it, when a vision appeared to him which revealed the treachery and diabolical intention of his mistress. To test the truth of the vision, he gave the dinner intended for himself to his faithful collie; the poor brute writhed, and died soon after in the greatest agony.

The following version is supplied by Mr Macintyre, teacher, Arpafeelie: – Although the various accounts as to the manner in which Coinneach Odhar became gifted with second sight differ in some respects, yet they generally agree in this, that it was acquired while he was engaged in the humble occupation of cutting peats or divots, which were in his day, and still are in many places, used as fuel throught the Highlands of Scotland. On the occasion referred to, being somewhat fatigued, he lay down, resting his head upon a little knoll, and waited the arrival of his wife with his dinner, whereupon he fell fast asleep. On awaking, he felt something hard under his head, and examining the cause of the uneasiness, discovered a small round stone with a hole through the middle. He picked it up, and looking through it, saw by the aid of this prophetic stone that his wife was coming to him with a dinner consisting of sowans and milk, polluted, though unknown to her, in a manner which, as well as several other particulars connected with it, we forbear to mention. But Coinneach found that though this stone was the means by which a supernatural power had been conferred upon him, it had, on its very first application, deprived him of the sight of that eye with which he looked through it, and he continued ever afterwards 'cam', or blind of an eye.

It would appear from this account that the intended murderer made use of the Seer's wife to convey the poison to her own husband, thus adding to her diabolical and murderous intention, by making her who would feel the loss the keenest, the medium by which her husband was to lose his life.

Hugh Miller, in his *Scenes and Legends in the North of Scotland*, says: – When serving as a field labourer with a wealthy clansman who resided somewhere near Brahan Castle, he made himself so formidable to the clansman's wife by his shrewd, sarcastic humour, that she resolved on destroying him by poison. With this design, she mixed a preparation of noxious herbs with his food when he was one day employed in digging turf in a solitary morass, and brought it to him in a pitcher. She found him lying asleep on one of those conical fairy hillocks which abound in some parts of the Highlands, and, her courage failing her, instead of awaking him, she set down the pitcher by his side and returned home. He woke shortly after, and, seeing the food, would have begun his repast, but feeling something press heavily against his heart, he opened his waistcoat and found a beautiful smooth stone, resembling a pearl, but much larger, which had apparently been dropped into his breast while he slept. He gazed at it in admiration, and became conscious as he gazed, that a strange faculty of seeing the future as distinctly as the present, and men's real designs and motives as clearly as their actions, was miraculously imported to him; and it is well for him that he should become so knowing at such a crisis, for the first secret he became acquainted with was that of the treachery practised against him by his mistress.

Hugh Miller was born in Cromarty in 1802, the son of a sailor. He began life as a stone-mason and bank clerk, was to become a geologist of world renown, and, in 1840, the Edinburgh editor of the Christian paper, *The Witness*, and eventually a powerful influence in Scotland.

His first love was geology and he is still recognised as one of the early experts in this field. It was through his writing that the Black Isle and Cromarty in particular became widely known, not only geologically but also socially and historically. His thatched cottage, built by a buccaneer ancestor in 1650 is now a museum preserved by the National Trust for Scotland and contains many of his fossil finds and memorabilia. Apart from his geological and autobiographical books, *Scenes and Legends of the North of Scotland* published in 1835 contains a comprehensive collection of old folklore stories connected with east Ross-shire.

He calls the Brahan Seer 'Kenneth Ore, a Highlander of Ross-shire, who lived some time in the seventeenth century' and, after Alexander Mackenzie's quoted paragraph, goes on to say:

'But he derived little advantage from the faculty ever after, for he led, it is said till extreme old age, an unsettled, unhappy kind of life – wandering from place to place, a prophet only of evil, or of little trifling events, fitted to attract notice when they occurred, merely from the circumstance of their having been foretold.

'There was a time of evil, he said, coming over the Highlands, when all things would appear fair and promising, and yet be both bad in themselves, and the beginnings of what would prove worse. A road would be opened among the hills from sea to sea, and a bridge built over every stream; but the people would be degenerating as their country was growing better; there would be ministers among them without grace, and maidens without shame; and the clans would have become so heartless, that they would flee out of their country before an army of sheep. Moss and muir would be converted into corn-land and yet hunger press as sorely on the poor as ever. Darker days would follow, for there would arise a terrible persecution, during which a ford in the river Oikel, at the head of the Dornoch Firth, would render a passage over the dead bodies of men, attired in the plaid and bonnet; and on the hill of Finnbhein, in Sutherlandshire, a raven would drink her fill of human blood three times a day for three successive days. The greater part of this prophecy belongs to the future; but almost all his minor ones are said to have met their fulfilment. He predicted, it is affirmed, that there would be dram-shops at the end of almost every furrow; that a cow would calve on the top of the old tower of Fairburn; that a fox would rear a litter of cubs on the hearthstone of Castle Downie; that another animal of the same species, but as white as snow, would be killed on the western coast of Sutherlandshire; that a wild deer would be taken alive at Fortrose Point; that a rivulet in Western Ross would be dried up in winter; and that there would be a deaf Seaforth. But it would be much easier to prove that these events have really taken place than that they have been foretold. Some of his other prophecies are nearly as equivocal, it has been remarked, as the responses of the old oracles, and true merely in the letter, or in some hidden meaning capable of being elicited by only the events which they anticipated. He predicted, it is said, that the ancient Chanonry of Ross, which is still standing, would fall "full of Mackenzies", and as the floor of the building has been used, from time immemorial, as a burying-place by several powerful families of the name, it is supposed that the prophecy cannot fail, in this way, of meeting its accomplishment. He predicted too that a huge natural arch near the Storhead of Assynt would be thrown down, and with so terrible a crash that the cattle of Ledmore, a proprietor who lives twenty miles inland, would break from their fastenings at the noise. It so happened, however, says the story, that some of Ledmore's cattle, which were grazing on the lands of another proprietor, were housed within a few hundred yards of the arch when it fell. The prophet, shortly before his death, is said to have flung the white stone into a lake near Brahan, uttering as his last prediction, that it would be found many years after, when all his prophecies would be fulfilled, by a lame humpbacked mendicant.'

We have thus several accounts of the manner in which our prophet obtained possession of his remarkable stone, white or blue, with or without a hole through its centre, it matters little; that he did obtain it, we must assume to be beyond question; but it is a matter for consideration, and indeed open to considerable doubt, whether it had any real prophetic virtue. If Kenneth was really possessed of the power of prophecy he more than likely used the stone simply to impose upon the people, who would never believe him possessed of such a gift, unless they saw with their own eyes the means by which he exercised it.

We shall, as far as possible, give the Prophecies under the following headings – Those which might be attributed to great penetration and natural shrewdness; those which are still unfulfilled; those that are doubtful; and those which have been unquestionably fulfilled, or partly fulfilled.

Prophecies which Might be Attributed to Natural Shrewdness

He no doubt predicted many things which the unbeliever in his prophetic gifts may ascribe to great natural shrewdness. Among these may be placed his prophecy, 150 years before the Caledonian Canal was built, that ships would some day sail round the back of Tomnahurich Hill. A gentleman from Inverness sent for Coinneach to take down his prophecies. He wrote several of them, but when he heard this one, he thought it so utterly absurd and impossible, that he threw the manuscript of what he had already written into the fire, and gave up any further communication with the Seer. Mr Maclennan gives the following version of it: – 'Strange as it may seem to you this day, the time will come, and it is not far off, when full-rigged ships will be seen sailing eastward and westward by the back of Tomnahurich, near Inverness.' Mr Mackintyre supplies us with a version in the Seer's vernacular Gaelic: – *Thig an latha 's am faicear laraichean Sasunnach air an tarruing le srianan corcaich seachad air cul Tom-na-hiuraich.* (The day will come when English mares, with hempen bridles shall be led round the back of Tomnahurich.) It is quite possible that a man of penetration and great natural shrewdness might, from the appearance of the country, with its chain of great inland lakes, predict the future Caledonian Canal.

The construction of the Caledonian Canal through the Great Glen was an enormous feat of engineering enterprise. It was begun in 1803 as an attempt to provide a safe water passage for ships of the Royal Navy during the Napoleonic wars, but was not completed until 1822. Its designer, Thomas Telford, had scores of roads and bridges already to his credit, many of which still survive. Sailing ships had, however, great difficulty navigating the Great Glen in strong winds, so steam tugs were provided in 1840. The Canal was found to be too small for the new iron-hulled steam ships so it had to be reconstructed at a cost of £150,000 in 1847. Though never the financial and industrial success envisaged, the Canal was used by coasting vessels, fishing boats and Baltic traders, and at its busiest era four passenger steamers plied between Inverness and Glasgow, and a service was operated from Liverpool. Today only short cruises are provided for sightseers and monster-spotters on Loch Ness, and, apart from a few ocean-going yachts and motor-cruisers, the fishing boats have the Canal to themselves.

Among others which might safely be predicted, without the aid of any supernatural gift, are, 'that the day will come when there will be a road through the hills of Ross-shire from sea to sea, and a bridge upon every stream.' 'That the people will degenerate as their country improves.' 'That the clans will become so effeminate as to flee from their native country before an army of sheep.' Mr Macintyre supplies the following version of the latter: – Alluding possibly to the depopulation of the Highlands, Coinneach said 'that the day will come when the Big Sheep will overrun the country until they strike (meet) the northern sea'. Big sheep here is commonly understood to mean deer, but whether the words signify sheep or deer, the prophecy has been very strikingly fulfilled. The other two have also been only too literally fulfilled.

Mr Macintyre supplies another version, as follows: 'The day will come when the hills of Ross will be strewed with ribbons.' It is generally accepted that this prediction finds its fulfilment in the many good roads that now intersect the various districts of the country. Other versions are given, such as 'a ribbon on every hill, and a bridge on every stream' (*Raoban air gach cnoc agus drochaid air gach alltan*); 'a mill on every river and a white house on every hillock' (*Muillin air gach abhainn agus tigh geal air gach cnocan*); and 'that the hills of the country will be crossed with shoulder-halts' (*criosan guaille*). Since Kenneth's day mills were very common, and among the most useful industrial institutions of the country, as may be evidenced by the fact that, even to this day, the proprietors of lands, where such establishments were once located, pay Crown and Bishop's rents for them. And may we not discover the fulfilment of 'a white house on every hillock' in the many elegant shooting lodges, hotels and school-houses now found in every corner of the Highlands.

Compare these versions with the Isla Seer's alleged prediction: 'The day is coming when there will be a bridge on every burn and a white house on every headland in Isla.' The white house is so called in contrast to the 'black house', traditional dwelling of the Gael, a low turf-thatched, three-apartment cottage with central fire, blackened inside and out with peat reek. Today the brilliant whitewashed cottages of Wester Ross and the Isles are a striking feature of the landscape.

The Isla Seer is also alleged to have said, 'The time is coming when the sheep's tooth will take the coulter of the plough out of the ground in Isla.' This is Thomas the Rhymer's version, 'The teeth of the sheep shall lay the plough on the shelf.' According to tradition, Thomas the Rhymer was a Learmont of Ercildoune or Earlston in the Scottish borders, who lived some time in the thirteenth century. He was prophet, bard and hero of elfin adventure who, in order to add credence to his predictions, boasted of conversation with the Queen of the Fairies. He claimed he lived with her for seven years, though it seemed 'nought but the space of days three'. She rewarded him with a long roll of prophecies and gave him the gift of prediction.

If thou wilt spell or tales tell
Thomas, thou shalt never make lee.

Apart from his ability to foresee the future, he is remarkable as the earliest Scots romantic writer. The poem entitled *The Romance of Sir Tristem*, allegedly written by him, is thought to be the first piece of important literature from the north.

Mr Maclennan supplies the following: – There is opposite the shore at Findon, Ferrintosh, two sandbanks which were, in the time of the Seer, entirely covered over with the sea, even at the very lowest spring ebbs. Regarding these, Coinneach said, 'that the day will come, however distant, when these banks will form the coast line; and when that happens, know for a certainty that troublesome times are at hand'. 'These banks', our correspondent continues, 'have been visibly approaching, for many years back, nearer and nearer to the shore.' This is another of the class of predictions which might be attributed to natural shrewdness. It is being gradually fulfilled, and it may be well to watch for 'the troublesome times', and so test the powers of the Seer.

These sandbanks, situated on the south shore of the Cromarty Firth and part of the Conon river estuary are particularly noticeable since the completion in the late seventies of the causeway extension of the A9 across the Cromarty Firth. At low tide, they are a great gathering place for seals.

Other predictions of this class may occur as we proceed, but we have no hesitation in saying that, however much natural penetration and shrewdness might have aided Kenneth in predicting such as these, it would assist him little in prophesying 'that the day will come when Tomnahurich', or, as he called it, *Tom-na-sithichean*, or the Fairy Hill, 'will be under lock and key, and the Fairies secured within'. It would hardly assist him in foreseeing the beautiful and unique cemetery on the top of the hill, and the spirits (of the dead) chained within, as we now see it.

The two-hundred-foot eker of Tomnahurich dominates the city of Inverness. Sometimes called the Hill of Fairies, but more accurately the Hillock of the Yew Trees (*Tom na h-iubraich*), it has been the focal point of legends from the earliest days. It was believed to have been the last resting place of Fingal and his Feinnian warriors, who lie resting on their elbows waiting for someone strong enough to blow their great hunting-horn – the last trump – when they will rise up and conquer the world. The first recorded burial took place in May 1846, and, as if to add greater force to the prediction, the cemetery was surrounded by a fence and the gate locked every night.

Since the last edition of the 'Prophecies' appeared, our attention has been called to the following paragraph published in the *Inverness Advertiser*, in 1859; that is *before* it had been turned into a cemetery – 'Tomnahurich, the far-famed Fairies' Hill, has been sown with oats. According to tradition, the Brahan prophet who lived 200 years ago, predicted that ships with unfurled sails would pass and repass Tomnahurich; and further, that it would yet be placed under lock and key. The first part of the prediction was verified by the opening of the Caledonian Canal, and we seem to be on the eve of seeing the realization of the rest by the final closing up of the Fairies' Hill.' This paragraph was in print before the prediction was fulfilled.

Unfulfilled Prophecies

Kenneth foretold 'that, however unlikely it may now appear, the Island of Lews will be laid waste by a destructive war, which will continue till the contending armies, slaughtering each other as they proceed, shall reach Tarbert in Harris. In the Caws of Tarbert, the retreating host will suddenly halt; an onslaught, led by a left-handed Macleod, called Donald, son of Donald, son of Donald, will then be made upon the pursuers. The only weapon in this champion's hands will be a black sooty *cabar*, taken off a neighbouring hut; but his intrepidity and courage will overpower their pursuers. The Lews will then enjoy a long period of repose.' It has not hitherto been suggested that this prophecy has been fulfilled, and we here stake the reputation of our prophet upon its fulfilment, and that of the following predictions, which are still current throughout the Northern Counties of Scotland.

The translation of the original Gaelic is given by the Rev W. Matheson in his paper to the Gaelic Society of Inverness, 1968, as follows:

> Donald of the three Donalds,
> Son of Clan Macleod, a left-handed man,
> Using a sooty rafter from his neighbour's house,
> Will repulse the enemy in the Cadha.

Mr Matheson suggests that there is good evidence to suppose that this prediction has already been fulfilled. The place referred to as the Cadha in Harris is on the south side of East Loch Tarbert. In Alexander Mackenzie's periodical, the *Celtic Magazine*, there is an account of a feud between the Morrisons of Ness in Lewis and the Macleods of Harris. These happenings occurred probably in 1544 and 1545, when Domhnall Dubh was contesting the Lordship of the Isles. The prophecy is, therefore, older than the Brahan Seer and was either the utterance of an earlier prophet or came into circulation after the event.

Another, by which the faith of future generations may be tested, is the one in which he predicted 'that a Loch above Beauly will burst through its banks and destroy in its rush a village in its vicinity'. We are not aware that such a calamity as is here foretold has yet occurred, nor are we aware of the locality of the loch or the village.

In 1967, heavy rain caused the Hydro-Electric dam at Torachilty to overflow, thus forcing the river Conon to burst its banks. The subsequent flooding destroyed buildings, cattle and crops, and created havoc in the village of Conon Bridge, five miles north of Beauly. Since then flood precautions have been taken to prevent further serious damage.

We have received various versions of the, as yet, unfulfilled prediction regarding *Clach an t-Seasaidh*, near the Muir of Ord. This is an angular stone, sharp at the top, which at one time stood upright, and was of considerable height. It is now partly broken and lying on the ground. 'The day will come when the ravens will, from the top of it, drink their three fulls, for three successive days, of the blood of the Mackenzies.'

Mr Maclennan's version is: – 'The day will come when the ravens will drink their full of the Mackenzies' blood three times off the top of the *Clach Mhor*, and glad am I (continues the Seer) that I will not live to see that day, for a bloody and destructive battle will be fought on the Muir of Ord. A squint-eyed (cam), pox-pitted tailor will originate the battle; for men will become so scarce in those days that each of seven women will strive hard for the squint-eyed tailor's heart and hand, and out of this strife the conflict will originate.'

Mr Macintyre writes regarding these: – 'The prophecies that "the raven will drink from the top of *Clach an t-Seasaidh*, its full

41

of the blood of the Mackenzies for three successive days", and "that the Mackenzies would be so reduced in numbers, that they would be all taken in an open fishing boat (*scuta dubh*) back to Ireland from whence they originally came", remain still unfulfilled.'

In the Kintail versions of these predictions they are made to apply to the Macraes, who are to get so scarce that a cripple tailor of the name is to be in such request among the ladies as to cause a desperate battle in the district between themselves and the Maclennans, the result of which will be that a black fishing wherry or *scuta dubh* will carry back to Ireland all that remains of the clan Macrae, but no sooner do they arrive than they again return to Kintail. Before this was to take place, nine men of the name of Macmillan would arrive at manhood (assume their bonnets) in the district; assemble at a funeral at Cnoc-a-Chlachain in Kilduich, and originate a quarrel. At this exact period, the Macraes would be at the height of their prosperity in Kintail, and henceforth begin to lose their hold in the country of their ancestors. The Macmillans have actually met in this spot and originated a quarrel as predicted, although nothing could have been more unlikely, for in the Seer's day there was not a single one of the name in Kintail, nor for several generations after. It is somewhat remarkable to find that the Maclennans are at this very time actually supplanting the Macraes as foretold, for the last two of the ancient stock – the late tenants of Fernaig and Leachachan – who left the district have been succeeded in their holdings by Maclennans; and other instances of the same kind, within recent years, are well known.

At present, we are happy to say, there does not appear much probability of the Clan Mackenzie being reduced to such small dimensions as would justify us in expecting the fulfilment of the *scuta dubh* part of the prophecy on a very early date. If the prediction, however, be confined in its application to the Mackenzies of Seaforth, it may be said to have been already almost fulfilled. We have, indeed, been told that this is a fragment of the unfulfilled prophecy uttered by Coinneach regarding the ultimate doom and total extinction of the Seaforths, and which we have been as yet unable to procure in detail. It was, however, known to Bernard Burke, who makes the following reference to it: – 'He (the Seer) uttered it in all its horrible length; but I at present suppress the last portion of it, which is as yet unfulfilled. Every other part of the prediction has most literally and most accurately come to pass, but let us earnestly hope that the course of future events may at length give the lie to the avenging curse of the Seer. The last clause of the prophecy is well known to many of those versed in Highland family tradition, and I trust that it may remain unfulfilled.'

One of our correspondents presumes that the mention of *Clach an t-Seasaidh* refers to the remains of a Druidical circle to be seen still on the right and left of the turnpike road at Windhill, near Beauly. As a sign whereby to know when the latter prophecy would be accomplished, Coinneach said 'that a mountain-ash tree will grow out of the walls of Fairburn Tower, and when it becomes large enough to form a cart axle, these things will come to pass'. Not long ago, a party informed us that a mountain-ash, or rowan-tree, was actually growing out of the tower walls, and was about the thickness of a man's thumb.

A different version of this prophecy is known locally, and states that a bird would plant a rowan tree on the top of Fairburn Tower and that when it grew to the thickness of an axle tree, the glory of the Seaforths would rise again. The tree was growing on the north-west face of the tower at the turn of the century and achieved some girth by 1921, when Stewart Mackenzie, a descendant of the last Lord Seaforth through his eldest daughter, was rewarded for his wartime services by the revival of the old family title. This too was to expire in due course as there was no male heir. The rowan tree died in the summer of 1957.

Various other unfulfilled predictions of the Seer remain to be noticed. One is regarding *Clach an Tiompain*, a well-known stone in the immediate vicinity of the far-famed Strathpeffer Wells. It is, like *Clach an t-Seasaidh*, an upright, pillar-looking stone, which, when struck, makes a great hollow sound or echo, and hence its designation, the literal meaning of which is the 'stone of the hollow sound or echo'. Coinneach said 'that the day will come when ships will ride with their cables attached to *Clach an Tiompain*'. It is perhaps superfluous to point out that this has not yet come to pass; and we could only imagine two ways in which it was possible to happen, either by a canal being made through the valley of Strathpeffer, passing in the neighbourhood of the Clach, or by the removal of the stone some day by the authorities of *Baile Chail* to Dingwall pier. They may feel disposed to thus aid the great prophet of their country to secure the position as a great man, which we now claim in his behalf.

A local prophecy attributed to the Brahan Seer and quoted by Otta Swire in *The Highlands and their Legends* (1963) stated that when five spires should rise in Strathpeffer, ships would sail over the village and anchor to them. When, in the early years of this century it was proposed that an Episcopal church should be built in Strathpeffer, the inhabitants presented a petition to the rector asking that he should not include a spire in the new building for fear of the prophecy's fulfilment. Eventually, however, both church and spire were erected without mishap. Then, shortly after the First World War, a small airship made an appearance at the Strathpeffer Games. It dropped a grapnel which became entangled in one of the spires, thus fulfilling the prophecy in an original but harmless way!

While the first edition was going through the press we visited Knockfarrel, in the immediate vicinity of Loch Ussie, and we were told of another way in which this prediction might be fulfilled so peculiar that, although it is altogether improbable, nay impossible, that it can ever take place, we shall reproduce it.

Knockfarrel is one in a line of three great Iron Age defence sites, the other two being at Craig Phadraig in Inverness and the Ord Hill, Kessock. It is a fine example of an Iron Age vitrified fort, built before the use of lime as a matrix. When excavated in 1774, the walls were found to be twenty-three feet high, but today only the foundations can be seen. There are many legends connected with this ancient site. It was believed to have been a stronghold of Fingal and his warriors, and one day, so the story goes, while they were hunting on the shores of the

Cromarty Firth, their womenfolk decided to play a trick on the unpopular Conon who was left in charge. Finding him asleep outside the fort, they staked his seven braids of hair to the ground, ran off and rang the alarm bell. Conon, leaping up, left half his scalp behind. Mad with rage and pain, he drove the women into the fort, set fire to it and destroyed them all.

Having found our way to the top of this magnificent and perfect specimen of a vitrified fort, we were so struck with its great size, that we carefully paced it, and found it to be one hundred and fifty paces in length, with a uniform width of forty, both ends terminating in a semi-circle, from each of which projected for a distance of sixty paces, vitrified matter, as if it were originally a kind of promenade, thus making the whole length of the structure two hundred and seventy yards, or thereabout. On the summit of the hill we met two boys herding cows, and as our previous experience taught us that boys, as a rule – especially herd boys – are acquainted with the traditions and places of interest in the localities they frequent, we were curious enough to ask them if they ever heard of Coinneach Odhar in the district, and if he ever said anything regarding the fort on Knockfarrel. They directed us to what they called 'Fingal's Well', in the interior of the ruined fort, and informed us that this well was used by the inhabitants of the fortress 'until Fingal, one day, drove them out, and placed a large stone over the well, which has ever since kept the water from oozing up, after which he jumped to the other side of the (Strathpeffer) valley'. There being considerable rains for some days previous to our visit, water could be seen in the 'well'. One of the boys drove down a stick until it struck the stone, producing a hollow sound which unmistakably indicated the existence of a cavity beneath. 'Coinneach Odhar foretold', said the boy, 'that if ever that stone was taken out of its place, Loch Ussie would ooze up through the well and flood the valley below to such an extent that ships could sail up to Strathpeffer and be fastened to *Clach an Tiompain*; and this would happen after the stone had fallen three times. It has already fallen twice,' continued our youthful informant, 'and you can now see it newly raised, strongly

and carefully propped up, near the end of the doctor's house.'
And so it is, and can still be seen, on the right, a few paces from
the roadside, as you proceed up to the Strathpeffer Wells.

Now known as the Eagle Stone, this has throughout the centuries
gathered a host of legends. One states that this was the site where the
Munros and other clans met Donald of the Isles on his way to the
Battle of Harlaw in 1411, and turned him from his course so that he
was forced to take another route. Called more correctly *Clach àn
Tuindain*, which means the 'Stone of the Turning', it was said to have
been erected by the Munros after another battle with Mackenzies and
inscribed with their crest – the eagle – in memory of the slain. It is now
known to be of far greater antiquity, inscribed with Pictish symbols,
one of a pair perhaps with the Gneiss Monolith, similarly carved,
which may be seen in the churchyard of St Clement's Church in
Dingwall. The Eagle Stone has already been removed at least twice and
on the second occasion the Cromarty Firth is said to have flooded up to
the old County Buildings in Dingwall. Today it is a well sign-posted
feature of Strathpeffer, firmly cemented into place and protected by a
fence, recognised for what it is, an important Pictish Class 1 symbol
stone dating probably from the sixth or seventh centuries AD.

We think it right to give this – a third – with the other versions,
for probably the reader will admit that the one is just as likely to
happen as the other. We can quite understand Kenneth prophesying that the sea would yet reach Strathpeffer; for to anyone standing where we did, on the summit of Knockfarrel, the bottom of
the valley appears much lower than the Cromarty Firth beyond
Dingwall, and it looks as if it might, any day, break through the
apparently slender natural embankment below Tulloch Castle,
which seemed, from where we stood, to be the only obstruction
in its path. We need, however, hardly inform the reader in the
district that the bottom of the Strathpeffer valley is, in reality,
several feet above the present sea level.

Another prediction is that concerning the Canonry of Ross,
which is still standing – 'The day will come when, full of the
Mackenzies, it will fall with a fearful crash.' This may come to
pass in several ways. The Canonry is the principal burying-place

of the Clan, and it may fall when full of dead Mackenzies, or when a large concourse of the Clan is present at the funeral of a great chief.

The Chanonry of Ross was the old name for the royal burgh of Fortrose in the Black Isle, but here refers to its ruined cathedral, for many centuries centre of the Diocese of Ross. Started about 1250 and not fully completed until c.1500, Euphemia, Countess of Ross made a grant of land for the support 'of the chapel of St Boniface adjacent to the town of Rosmarkyn' in 1379. Now nothing remains of the main portion of the cathedral except for the ground plan marked out in gravel and Euphemia's beautiful south aisle. This is literally full of 'dead Mackenzies' for it became the burial vault for the Seaforth and Coul Mackenzies. Here may be seen the memorial tablets to Francis Humberstone Mackenzie 'the last of the Seaforths' and his four sons, whose end was foretold by the Brahan Seer more than a century before their deaths.

The dilapidation of the cathedral began soon after the Reformation, when the old hierarchy was no longer able to pay for its upkeep. In 1572, James VI granted to his treasurer, Lord Ruthven, 'the haill led quhairwith the Cathedral Kirk of Ros is thickit'. Although Cromwell's men under General Carr have been blamed for its final destruction, they were responsible only for removing the already-fallen stones to build a new citadel at Inverness. A few years later, Kenneth, the third Earl of Seaforth, set fire to what remained of the roof. Alexander Brodie recalled in his diary for 6 November 1662, 'I heard that Earl Seaforth by a shot of a gun had burnt the Kirk of Channonrie, other houses there being at the same time burnt by accident'. The Earl was apparently shooting pigeons on the Kirk green.

In 1977 a further prediction came to light which may or may not have been invented after the occasion. 'When there is a wedding in the ruins of the cathedral, Fortrose will become a town of widows and the cemetery full to overflowing.' In 1975 there had been a wedding in the ruins. At the same time the cemetery in Fortrose was full and another site in consideration on the edge of the town. For the first half of 1977, the local registrar recorded twice as many deaths as usual. These three facts somehow added up to a prediction which was to make headlines in the *Sunday Times*. There are many who assert that the prediction was known before the event. Unfortunately it was never written down.

'When two false teachers shall come across the seas who will revolutionize the religion of the land, and nine bridges shall span the river Ness, the Highlands will be overrun by ministers without grace and women without shame,' is a prediction which some maintain has all the appearance of being rapidly fulfilled at this moment. It has been suggested that the two false teachers were no other than the great evangelists, Messrs Moody and Sankey, who, no doubt, from Coinneach Odhar's standpoint of orthodoxy, who must have been a Roman Catholic or an Episcopalian, attempted to revolutionize the religion of the Highlands. If this be so, the other portions of the prophecy are looming not far off in the immediate future. We have already eight bridges on the Ness – the eighth has only been finished last year – and the ninth is almost finished. If we are to accept the opinions of certain of the clergy themselves, 'ministers without grace' are becoming the rule, and as for a plenitude of 'women without shame', ask any ancient matron, and she will at once tell you that Kenneth's prophecy may be held to have been fulfilled in that particular any time within the last half century. *Gleidh sinne!!*

It is possible the following may have something to do with the same calamity in the Highlands. Mr Maclennan says: – With reference to some great revolution which shall take place in the country, Coinneach Odhar said that 'before that event shall happen, the water of the river Beauly will cease to run. On one of these occasions a salmon, having shells instead of scales, will be found in the bed of the river.' This prophecy has been in part fulfilled, for the Beauly has on two occasions ceased to run and a salmon of the kind mentioned has been found in the bed of the river.

Mr Macintyre gives another version: – 'When the river Beauly is dried up three times, and a "scaly salmon" or royal sturgeon, is caught in the river, that will be a time of great trial.' (*Nuair a thraoghas abhainn na Manachain tri uairean, agus a ghlacair Bradan Sligeach ar grunnd na h-aibhne, 's ann an sin a bhitheas an deuchainn ghoirt.*) The river has been already dried up twice, the last time in 1826, and a *Bradan Sligeach*, or royal sturgeon, measuring nine feet in length, has been caught in the estuary of the Beauly about two years ago.

The following is one which we trust may never be realized in all its details, though some may be disposed to think that signs are not wanting of its ultimate fulfilment: – 'The day will come when the jaw-bone of the big sheep, or *caoirich mhora*, will put the plough on the rafters (*air an aradh*); when sheep shall become so numerous that the bleating of the one shall be heard by the other from Conchra in Lochalsh to Bun-da-Loch in Kintail, they shall be at their height in price, and henceforth will go back and deteriorate, until they disappear altogether, and be so thoroughly forgotten that a man finding the jaw-bone of a sheep in a cairn, will not recognize it, or be able to tell what animal it belonged to. The ancient proprietors of the soil shall give place to strange merchant proprietors, and the whole Highlands will become one huge deer forest; the whole country will be so utterly desolated and depopulated that the crow of a cock shall not be heard north of Druim-Uachdair; the people will emigrate to Islands now un-known, but which shall yet be discovered in the boundless oceans after which the deer and other wild animals in the huge wilderness shall be exterminated and browned by horrid *black* rains (*siantan dubha*). The people will then return and take undisturbed poss-ession of the lands of their ancestors.'

A shorter version of this well-known prophecy is quoted locally: 'Sheep shall eat men, men will eat sheep, the black rain will eat all things; in the end old men shall return from new lands.'

This prophecy is the one most often quoted and still feared in the Highlands today, and not without reason. In it, Coinneach Odhar saw the history of the Highlands from the time of the evictions through the present day and into the future that lies ahead. Shortly after Culloden, the landowners and clan chiefs began to replace the crofters and their old form of agriculture with sheep and shepherds from the south. This caused unbelievable hardship to the evicted tenants, many of whom were forced to emigrate to Newfoundland and New Zealand, islands unknown to the Seer.

In their turn many of the old clan chiefs were forced to sell their estates to the new rich industrialists or to Lowland and English sheep-farmers, who took up leases of glens evacuated during the clearances. Soon vast tracts of land became the property of absentee landlords, who stocked the mountains with game in order to indulge themselves in an orgy of slaughter for a few months in the year.

The desolation and depopulation of the Highlands which started after Culloden continued right up to the mid-twentieth century. Strong efforts have been made by the various Highland Councils, Development and Enterprise organisations to bring employment and prosperity to the north and they are proving successful. Apart from the major establishment of oil-rig platforms at Nigg and Ardersier, there are thousands of flourishing smaller ventures which, it is hoped, will keep the young people in the Highlands and encourage others to return.

Some fear that the time of the horrid black rains may be close at hand. Until recently some believed that this might mean nuclear fall-out. Others talked of an underwater explosion in the oil fields in the North Sea, but most Highlanders today associate the black rain with pollution.

We have yet to see the realization of the following: – 'A dun, hornless cow (supposed to mean a steamer) will appear in the Minch (off Carr Point, in Gairloch), and make a *geum*, or bellow, which will knock the six chimneys off Gairloch House.' (*Thig bo mhaol odhar a steach an t-Aite-mor agus leigeas i geum aiste 'chuireas na se beannagan dheth an Tigh Dhige.*) Gairloch House, or the Tigh Dige of Coinneach's day, was the old house which stood in the park on the right, as you proceed from the bridge in the direction of the present mansion. The walls were of wattled twigs, wicker work, or plaited twig hurdles, thatched with turf or divots, and surrounded with a deep ditch, which could, in time of approaching danger, be filled with water from the river, hence the name *Tigh Dige*, House of the Ditch. It has been suggested that the Seer's prediction referred to this stronghold, but a strong objection to this view appears in the circumstance that the ancient citadel had no chimneys to fall off. The present mansion is, however, also called the Tigh Dige, and it has the exact number of chimneys – six.

During the search for Prince Charles Edward Stuart, a man-of-war entered Gairloch Bay and the captain invited the owner of Tigh Dige, Sir Alexander Mackenzie, to come on board. He got a rude answer for his trouble, and the angry captain fired a broadside at the house in reply. Although there is no mention of the chimneys having fallen, an eighteen-pound cannonball was found lodged in the gable end.

This story is to be found in Osgood Mackenzie's book, *A Hundred Years in the Highlands*, and is thought to account for the prophecy's fulfilment.

'The day will come when a river in Wester Ross shall be dried up.' 'The day will come when there shall be such dire persecution and bloodshed in the county of Sutherland, that people can ford the river Oykel dryshod, over dead men's bodies.' 'The day will come when a raven, attired in plaid and bonnet, will drink his full of human blood on *Fionn-bheinn*, three times a day, for three successive days.'

'A battle will be fought at Ault-nan-Torcan, in the Lewis, which will be a bloody one indeed. It will truly take place, though the time may be far hence, but woe to the mothers of sucklings that day. The defeated host will continue to be cut down till it reaches Ard-a-chaolais (a place nearly seven miles from Ault-nan-Torcan), and there the swords will make terrible havoc.' This has not yet occurred.

This prophecy is quoted more fully by Mr Matheson in his paper to the Gaelic Society, Inverness:

It is on the day of Allt nan Torcan
that injury will be done to the women of Lewis;
between Eidseal and Aird a Chaolais
the sword edges will be struck.

They'll come, they'll come, 'tis not long till there
will come ashore at Portnaguran
those who will reduce the country to a sorry state:
alas for the woman with a little child –
everyone of the Clan MacAulay
will have his head dashed against a stone,
and she herself will be slain along with him.

This, says Mr Matheson, might describe a battle in which the MacAulays were massacred at a place called Allt nan Torcan on the road from Stornoway to Uig. It is not sensible to look into the future for the fulfilment of such a prediction, but it might well have happened in the remote past. The MacAulays were at one time practically exterminated in a battle, the only survivor being the chief's youngest son, Iain Ruadh, and his illegitimate half-brother. Iain was the grandfather of Domhnall Cam, chief of Clan MacAulay in the early seventeenth century. This would place the MacAulay massacre, still spoken of in Uig, as long ago as the early sixteenth century. An army under the command of the Earl of Huntly invaded Lewis in 1506 to quell a rebellion, and the MacLeods, who were closely allied to the MacAulays, were defeated.

Speaking of what should come to pass in the parish of Lochs, he said – 'At bleak Runish in Lochs, they will spoil and devour, at the foot of the crags, and will split heads by the score.'

This prophecy of murder in Raanish in the district of Lochs, Lewis, has also been closely investigated by Mr Matheson and is thought by him to have already been fulfilled. One of the early Mackenzie settlers in Lewis was a certain Iain Og who went to live at Raanish. One night in May 1616, a band of Macleods attacked and killed him. His widow complained to the Privy Council that her husband had been murdered 'in his naked bed'.

He is also said to have predicted 'that the day will come when the raven will drink its three fulls of the blood of the Clan Macdonald on the top of the Hills of Minaraidh in Parks, in the parish of

Lochs.' This looks as if the one above predicted about the Mackenzies had been misapplied to the Macdonalds.

Here again, according to Mr Matheson, there is a possible explanation for this prediction about bloodshed in Park in Lewis. In 1566 and the following years, Lewis was being harried by the Macdonalds under Hugh, who landed at Loch Seaforth and created havoc on the west side of the island. However, the Lewismen rallied under a Macleod and defeated the invaders at the Barvas river, and those who survived ran for their boats with the Macleods at their heels. There was another fight at Park and the result was that out of seventy-two Macdonalds, only twenty escaped alive.

If these explanations are credible, it is obvious that the Coinneach Odhar of Alexander Mackenzie's book could not have uttered the prophecies, as all three occurred before his alleged dates.

'The day will come when there shall be a laird of Tulloch who will kill four wives in succession, but the fifth shall kill him.'

Duncan Davidson, the Laird of Tulloch known locally as 'the Stag', had five wives who between them bore him eighteen children; and he was said to have had at least thirty illegitimate offspring in the district. One of his wives was his daughter-in-law's youngest sister, which, as both had children, caused complicated family relationships. He died of pneumonia caught while attending a function in Edinburgh, and was survived by his fifth wife.

It was his letter to Alexander Mackenzie dated May 1878, that helped to authenticate the Seaforth prediction. The prophecy about himself was in circulation long before his first marriage.

Tulloch Castle, now a hotel, dates from the sixteenth century, though it has been much changed and added to over the years. It belonged to the Bain family until 1760, when it passed to the Davidsons.

Regarding the battle of Ard-nan-Ceann, at Benbecula, North Uist, he said – 'Oh, Ard-nan-Ceann, Ard-nan-Ceann, glad am I that I will not be at the end of the South Clachan that day, when the young men will be weary and faint; for Ard-nan-Ceann will be the scene of a terrible conflict.'

This prophecy is more accurately translated from the Gaelic by Mr Matheson as follows:

Aird nan Ceann, Aird nan Ceann,
I am glad I'll not be there,
at the head of Clachan a Deas
where the men will be faint,
and the hot hard battle will be fought.

'A severe battle will be fought at the (present) Ardelve market stance, in Lochalsh, when the slaughter will be so great that people can cross the ferry over dead men's bodies. The battle will be finally decided by a powerful man and his five sons, who will come across from the Strath (the Achamore district).'

Coinneach said – 'When a holly bush (or tree) shall grow out of the face of the rock at Torr-a-Chuilinn (Kintail) to a size sufficiently large to make a shaft for a *carn-slaoid* (sledge-cart) a battle will be fought in the locality.'

It seems reasonable to suppose that this and the previous prediction have already been fulfilled in the remote past.

'When Loch Shiel, in Kintail, shall become so narrow that a man can leap across it, the salmon shall desert the Loch and the River Shiel.' We are told that the Loch is rapidly getting narrower at a particular point, by the action of the water on the banks and bottom, and that if it goes on as it has done in recent years it can easily be leaped at no distant date. Prudence would suggest a short lease of these Salmon Fishings.

He also predicted that a large stone, standing on the hill opposite Scallisaig farm-house, in Glenelg, 'will fall and kill a man'. This boulder is well known to people in the district, and the prophecy is of such a definite character, that there cannot possibly be any mistake about its meaning or its fulfilment should such a calamity ever unfortunately take place.

This stone is still standing, though somewhat precariously. If it were to become dislodged, it would fall on the Glenelg road below.

The following predictions as yet unfulfilled or partially fulfilled have been collected since the 1977 edition of this book. They are worth recording because they reflect the fears and prejudices of Highlanders in the past and a dislike of change that is still very much part of the present.

'The day will come when *Suidhe Dhearg* (Red Seat) in the Torridon mountains will fall on Fasag and the only survivor will be a woman in a red petticoat holding a red cockerel.'

This prediction was quoted recently in the village of Fasag which is tucked tightly under the steep and towering Torridon mountains in a very vulnerable position. In the old days no red cocks were allowed to survive in the village.

'A pinnacle of rock in Reraig will fall and kill a red-haired woman and child.' Contributed by Mrs M. Mackay of Lochalsh.

Although the workmen employed to improve the A87 between Ardelve and Balmacara in Wester Ross continually reported sick in respect of the prediction, the rock was blasted away and all that remains now is the base which can be found in the grass and whin at the edge of the new road. The 'red-haired woman' was thought to have been one of the 'Royal Stewarts of Plockton' a family of travelling folk famous for their red hair and the fact that they were continually on the road.

'The old bridge at Bonar Bridge will go down with a red-headed fishwife on it.'

The old bridge was swept away by floods in 1892 but whether the red-headed fishwife was on it at the time is not recorded. The prophecy was heard in 1984 when another improved bridge was at the planning stage. Red, the colour of blood, used to be considered magical in the Highlands.

'If any man should harm the Whispering Rock at Brahan and if his hair be fair, he will died a lingering death within six months.'

Quoted in the Dingwall district and recorded in the press, this prophecy came to prominence in 1984 when the rock – thought in past times to be a haunt of the fairies – was found to be obstructing the proposed road improvements between Dingwall and Contin (A835). Workmen from the area refused to touch it and in the end explosives were used by outside contractors and the rock blasted out of existence.

'When the Bornish Stone falls in South Uist, little green men will over-run the island.'

When the army established a base in the area the prophecy was remembered and local opposition strong as the 'little green men' were thought to be soldiers in uniform. It was alleged that certain officials one dark night tried to dislodge the stone but they were not successful and the ancient monolith still stands.

'The one-legged monster will leave Loch Kishorn and go twice below the water breathing fire and the third time will spell disaster in the German ocean.'

This prediction was quoted by the oil-rig workers on Loch Kishorn in the early eighties. It would seem to refer to the Ninian Central Platform constructed there. This was a monolithic structure which submerged twice before its final positioning and it did breath fire from the flare stack.

'When the Ullapool Ferry crosses to Stornoway, it will sink with all lives lost.'

This prediction was repeated in Ullapool in 1982 soon after the first official ferry was started. A variation which states that 'The *Isle of Lewis* will sink without trace or survivors' came into prominence in 1995 when on July 31 the Caledonian MacBrayne shipping company launched a fine modern vessel called the *Isle of Lewis* to follow the same route. The prediction swept through the island and the press was full of dire warnings but so far all is well. There are people however who refuse to travel by the ferry for fear of the prophecy.

'Birds will pick the bones of Caithness folk.'

This is a fragment of prophecy heard in Wick in the early eighties and is thought to be connected with the nuclear installation at Dounreay.

'When a huge ball rises up in Caithness, the North of Scotland will be devastated by black rain.' This was quoted in Wick in 1986 and referred to the erection of the nuclear power station at Dounreay. The 'black rain' was thought then to refer to nuclear fall-out.

'The bridge over the railway station at Dunrobin will collapse and kill the Duke of Sutherland.'

Quoted in Brora, this prophecy was evidently known to the fifth Duke who invariably got off the train at Golspie and drove to Dunrobin Castle!

'When it is possible to walk from England to France dry-shod, then England and Scotland will become a divided nation again.'

This splendid prediction was quoted in Elgin in 1990 by the niece of a woman who first heard it in Petty primary school (near Inverness) in 1929. It is thought to refer to the building of the Channel Tunnel. The Scottish Nationalist Party eagerly embraced the prophecy, and with Scotland about to get its own Parliament again, it looks as if it may soon be – partially at least – fulfilled.

Prophecies as to the Fulfilment of which there is a Doubt

'When a magpie (pitheid) shall have made a nest for three successive years in the gable of the Church of Ferrintosh, the church will fall when full of people,' is one of those regarding which we find it difficult to decide whether it has been already fulfilled or not. Mr Macintyre, who supplies this version, adds the following remarks: – The Church of Ferrintosh was known at an earlier period as the Parish Church of Urquhart and Loggie. Some maintain that this prediction refers to the Church of Urray. Whether this be so or not, there were circumstances connected with the Church of Ferrintosh in the time of the famous Rev Dr Macdonald, which seemed to indicate the beginning of the fulfilment of the prophecy, and which led to very alarming consequences. A magpie actually did make her nest in the church gable, exactly as foretold. This, together with a rent between the church wall and the stone stairs which led up to the gallery, seemed to favour the opinion that the prophecy was on the eve of being accomplished, and people felt uneasy when they glanced upon the ominous nest, the rent in the wall, and the crowded congregation, and remembered Coinneach's prophecy, as they walked into the church to hear the Doctor. It so happened one day that the church was unusually full of people, insomuch that it was found necessary to connect the ends of the seats with planks, in order to accommodate them all. Unfortunately, one of those temporary seats was either too weak, or too heavily burdened: it snapped in two with a loud report and startled the audience. Coinneach

Odhar's prophecy flashed across their minds, and a simultaneous rush was made by the panic-struck congregation to the door. Many fell, and were trampled underfoot, while others fainted, being seriously crushed and bruised.

Among a rural population, sayings and doings, applicable to a particular parish, crop up, and, in after times, are applied to occurrences in neighbouring parishes. Having regard to this, may it not be suggested that, what is current locally in regard to Ferrintosh and Coinneach's sayings, may only be a transcript of an event now a matter of history in a parish on the northern side of the Cromarty Firth. We refer to the destruction of the Abbey Church at Fearn by lightning, 10 October, 1742.

This Abbey was originally a Premonstratensian Monastery, founded in Edderton in the early thirteenth century. The Abbot and monks disapproved of the land there and asked to be transferred to the present site at Fearn where the fields were as fertile as the best in Scotland. One of Fearn's most famous Abbots was Patrick Hamilton, a first preacher of the Reformation who died a martyr's death in St Andrews in 1528. A later Abbot was Nicholas Ross, close relative of Alexander Ross of Balnagown, who, in 1560, attended the Reformation Parliament. The Rosses of Balnagowan were traditionally buried in the Abbey.

We have never seen a detailed account of this sad accident in print, and have no doubt the reader will be glad to have a graphic description of it from the pen of Bishop Forbes, the famous author of the *Jacobite Memoirs*, who visited his diocese of Ross and Caithness in the summer of 1762. This account is taken from his unpublished MS Journal, now the property of the College of Bishops of the Scottish Episcopal Church, and presently in the hands of the Rev F. Smith, Arpafeelie, who has kindly permitted us to make the following extract: –

'The ruinous Church of Ferne was of old an Abbacy of White Friars (see Keith's Catalogue, p. 247). The roof of flagstones, with part of a side wall, was beat down in an instant by thunder and lightning on Sunday, October 10th, 1742, and so crushed and bruised forty persons, that they were scarcely to be discovered, who or what they were, and therefore, were buried promiscuously, without any manner of distinction. The gentry, having luckily their seats in the niches, were saved from the sudden crash, as was the preacher by the sounding-boards falling upon the pulpit, and his bowing down under it. Great numbers were wounded (see *Scot's Magazine* for 1742, p 485). But there is a most material circumstance not mentioned, which has been carefully concealed from the publishers, and it is this: By a Providential event, this was the first Sunday that the Rev and often-mentioned Mr Stewart, had a congregation near Cadboll, in view of Ferne, whereby many lives were saved, as the kirk was far from being so throng as usual, and that he and his people, upon coming out from worship, and seeing the dismal falling-in just when it happened, hastened with all speed to the afflictive spot, and dragged many of the wounded out of the rubbish, whose cries would have pierced a heart of adamant. Had not this been the happy case, I speak within bounds when I say two, if not three, to one, would have perished. Some of the wounded died. This church had been a large and lofty building, as the walls are very high, and still standing.'

It has been suggested that the prediction was fulfilled by the falling to pieces of the Church at the Disruption; but we would be loath to stake the reputation of our prophet on this assumption.

Another, supposed by some to be fulfilled by the annual visits of the militia for their annual drill, is – 'That when a wood on the Muir of Ord grows to a man's height, regiments of soldiers shall be seen there drawn up in battle order.'

In connection with the battle, or battles, at Cille-Chriosd and the Muir of Ord, Mr Macintyre says: – The Seer foretold that '*Fear Ruadh an Uird* (the Red Laird of Ord) would be carried home, wounded, on blankets.' Whether this saying has reference to an event looming in the distant future, or is a fragment of a tradition regarding sanguinary events well known in the history of Cille-Chriosd, and of which a full and graphic account can be seen on pp 82–86 and 136–139, Vol I of the *Celtic Magazine*, it is impossible to say.

The legend referred to is now alleged to contain no truth, but has been part of Ross-shire folklore for many years. It concerns the small ruined Chapel at Gilchrist near Muir of Ord where the Macdonells of Glengarry were said to have set fire to the building while full of Mackenzie worshippers. The alleged tragedy originated in one of the many fights between the two clans over land, and both were said to be equally to blame. The chapel is the burial-ground of the Mackenzies of Ord.

Prophecies Wholly or Partly Fulfilled

There are several additional predictions which have been wholly or partly fulfilled. 'The day will come when the Mackenzies will lose all their possessions in Lochalsh, after which it will fall into the hands of an Englishman, who shall be distinguished by great liberality to his people, and lavish expenditure of money. He will have one son and two daughters; and, after his death, the property will revert to the Mathesons, its original possessors, who will build a Castle on Druim-a-Dubh, at Balmacarra.' The late Mr Lillingstone was an Englishman. He was truly distinguished for kindness and liberality to his tenants, and he had a son and two daughters, although, we are informed, he had been married for seventeen years before he had any family. When he came into possession, old people thought they discerned the fulfilment of a part of Kenneth's prediction in his person, until it was remarked that he had no family as predicted by the Seer. At last, a son and two daughters were successivly born to Mr Lillingstone. After his death, the son sold the whole of Lochalsh to Alexander Matheson, MP for the Counties of Ross and Cromarty, and, so far, the prediction has been realized. A castle was being built at Duncraig, a considerable distance from the spot predicted by the Seer; but if Kenneth is to be depended upon, a castle will yet be built by one of the Mathesons on Druim-a-Dubh, at Balmacarra. Had this prophecy been got up after the event, the reputation of the Seer would certainly not have been staked on the erection of another

castle in the remote future, when the Mathesons already possess
such a magnificent mansion at Duncraig.

Duncraig Castle with its stunning views of Plockton is owned by
Highland Council. For some years it was a domestic school attached to
the Inverness College but is now closed. It currently awaits a decision
as to its future.

During a recent visit to the Island of Raasay we received a peculiar
prediction regarding the Macleods from an old man there, over
eighty years of age, who remembered seven proprietors of Raasay,
and who sorely lamented the fulfilment of the prophecy, and the
decline of the good old stock, entirely in consequence of their own
folly and extravagance. Since then, we had the prediction repeated by a Kintail man in identical terms; and as it is hardly
translatable, we shall give it in the original vernacular: – *'Dar a
thig Mac-Dhomhnuill Duibh bàn; MacShimidh ceann-dearg; Sisealach claon ruadh; Mac-Coinnich mor bodhar; agus Mac-Gille-
challum cama-chasach, iar-ogha Ian bhig à Ruiga, 'se sin a Mac-
Gille-challum is miosa 'thainig na thig; cha bhi mi ann ri linn, 's
cha'n fhearr leam air a bhith.'* (When we shall have a fair-haired
Lochiel; a red-haired Lovat; a squint-eyes, fair-haired Chisholm;
a big deaf Mackenzie; and a bow-crooked-legged Mac-Gille-
challum, who shall be the great-grandson of John Beg, or Little
John, of Ruiga: that Mac-Gille-challum will be the worst that
ever came or ever will come; I shall not be in existence in his day,
and I have no desire that I should.) Ruiga is the name of a place
in Skye. When the last Macleod of Raasay was born, an old sage
in the district called upon his neighbour, and told him, with an
expression of great sorrow, that Mac-Gille-challum of Raasay now
had an heir, and his birth was a certain forerunner of the extinction of his house. Such an event as the birth of an heir had been
hitherto, in this as in all other Highland families, universally
considered an occasion for great rejoicing among the retainers.
The other old man was amazed, and asked the sage what he meant
by such unusual and disloyal remarks. 'Oh!' answered he, 'do you

not know that this is the grand-grandson of John Beg of Ruiga whom Coinneach Odhar predicted would be the worst of his race.' And so he undoubtedly proved himself to be, for he lost for ever the ancient inheritance of his house, and acted generally in such a manner as to fully justify the Seer's prediction; and what is still more remarkable, the Highland lairds, with the peculiar characteristics and malformations foretold by Kenneth, preceded or were the contemporaries of the last Mac-Gillie-challum of Raasay.

Here is a prediction of the downfall of another distinguished Highland family – Clan Ranald of the Isles. 'The day will come when the old wife with the footless stocking (*cailleach nam mogan*) will drive the Lady of Clan Ranald from Nunton House, in Benbecula.' We are informed that this was fulfilled when the Macdonalds took the farm of Nunton, locally known as 'Baile na Caillich'. Old Mrs Macdonald was in the habit of wearing these primitive articles of dress, and was generally known in the district as *Cailleach nam Mogan*. Clan Ranald and his lady, like many more of our Highland chiefs, ultimately went to the wall, and the descendants of the 'old wife with the footless stocking' occupied, and, for anything we know, still occupy the ancient residence of the long-distinguished race of Clan Ranald of the Isles.

The Macdonalds of Clanranald were the great family of Benbecula for many generations. Their downfall started with the death of the chief at the Battle of Sheriffmuir and was completed in 1745 when Prince Charles escaped to Nunton after Culloden. It was here that Flora Macdonald and Lady Clanranald dressed the Prince as 'Betty Burke', an Irish maid, so that he could escape to Skye. Shortly afterwards General Campbell arrested Clanranald, thus ending a long and glorious chiefdom. Eventually the line was to die out altogether. The family's last territorial possession was Castle Tioram on Loch Moidart. The *mogan*, or footless stocking, was a primitive form of footwear.

In the beginning of the seventeenth century, and during the Seer's lifetime, there lived in Kintail an old man – Duncan Macrae – who was curious to know by what means he should end his days.

Uig Sands in Lewis. The Seer was thought to have been brought up near here

Port of Ness, Lewis. Birthplace of the Seer according to the Bannatyne History of the Macleods

Dunvegan Castle, Isle of Skye, Seat of Clan Macleod

The Five Sisters of Kintail from Ratagan. Many of the Seer's prophecies originated from this area

Hugh Miller of Cromarty: stonemason, geologist and writer. He called the Seer a field labourer employed near Brahan Castle

Tomnahurich in Inverness, looking west. The Seer predicted its future as a cemetery

The Caledonian Canal at Muirton, Inverness. The Seer foresaw this when he said, 'The time will come when full-rigged ships will sail by the back of Tomnahurich'

The old Leanach Cottage, Culloden. The Seer foretold the last tragic battle to be fought on British soil

The Pump Room at Strathpeffer. The Seer predicted that 'crowds of pleasure and health seekers shall be seen thronging its portals'

The Eagle Stone, Strathpeffer, cemented in place to prevent a third fall

Fairburn Tower near Muir of Ord. In the days when it was a Mackenzie stronghold, the Seer predicted that a calf would be born in the top chamber

Kilcoy Castle. According to the Seer's prediction, it lay derelict for many years. It has recently been restored

Redcastle. Haunted and derelict, it also featured in the Seer's predictions

He applied to a local female seer, who informed him that he 'would die by the sword' (*le bàs a chlaidheamh*). This appeared so improbable in the case of such an old man, who had taken part in so many bloody frays and invariably escaped unhurt, that the matter was referred to the greater authority, Coinneach Odhar. He corroborated the woman, but still the matter was almost universally discredited in the district, and by none more so than by old Duncan himself. However, years after, conviction was forced upon them; for, according to the *Genealogy of the Macraes*, written by the Rev John Macrae, minister of Dingwall, who died in 1704 – 'Duncan being an old man in the year 1654, when General Monk, afterwards Duke of Albemarle, came to Kintail, retired from his house in Glenshiel to the hills, where, being found by some of the soldiers who had straggled from the body of the army in hopes of plunder, and who, speaking to him roughly, in a language he did not understand, he, like Old Orimanus, drew his sword, &c, and was immediately killed by them. This was all the blood that General Monk or his soldiers, amounting to 1500 men, had drawn, and all the opposition he met with, although the Earl of Middleton and Sir George Monro were within a few miles of them, and advertised of their coming, Seaforth having been sent by Middleton to the Isle of Skye and parts adjoining, to treat with the Macdonalds and the Macleods, &c.'

Regarding the evictions which would take place in the Parish of Petty, he said, 'The day will come, and it is not far off, when farm-steadings will be so few and far between, that the crow of a cock shall not be heard from the one steading to the other.' This prediction has certainly been fulfilled, for, in the days of the Seer there were no fewer than sixteen tenants on the farm of Morayston alone.

This prophecy is more correctly attributed to the Rev John Morrison, known as the Petty Seer, who was a prophet and visionary almost as well known as, and certainly better authenticated than, the Brahan Seer. He was Minister of the parish of Petty, which is situated between Culloden and Dalcross near Inverness, from 1759 to 1774. In this prophecy he predicts the Petty clearances as follows: 'Large as the

Ridge of Petty is and thickly as it is now populated, the day will come, and is not far off, when there will only be three smokes in it, and the crow of the cock at each cannot be heard, owing to the distance, at either of the others. After a time, however, the lands will again be divided, and the parish of Petty become as populous as it is at this day.'

Mr A. B. Maclennan, one of Alexander Mackenzie's main sources, collected and published the works and sayings of the Rev John Morrison under the title of *The Petty Seer*.

On the south of the bay, at Petty, is an immense stone, of at least eight tons weight, which formerly marked the boundary between the estates of Culloden and Moray. On 20 February 1799, it was mysteriously removed from its former position, and carried about 260 yards into the sea. It is supposed by some that this was brought about by an earthquake; others think that the stone was carried off by the action of ice, combined with the influence of a tremendous hurricane, which blew from the shore, during that fearful and stormy night. It was currently reported, and pretty generally believed at the time, that his Satanic Majesty had a finger in this work. Be that as it may, there is no doubt whatever that the Brahan Seer predicted 'that the day will come when the Stone of Petty, large though it is, and high and dry upon the land as it appears to people this day, will be suddenly found as far advanced into the sea as it now lies away from it inland, and no one will see it removed, or be able to account for its sudden and marvellous transportation.'

This prophecy, like the previous one, is also more correctly attributed to the Rev John Morrison, who allegedly cried out during a sermon: 'Ye sinful and stiff-necked people, God will, unless ye turn from your evil ways, sweep you ere long into the place of torment; and as a sign of the truth of what I say, *Clach Dubh an Abain*, large though it be, will be carried soon without human agency a considerable distance seawards.'

Twenty-six years later, this was to happen in a dramatic fashion. Anderson, in his *Guide to the Highlands*, writes, 'On the south side of the bay (of Petty) an immense stone, weighing at least eight tons, which marked the boundarie between the estates of Lord Moray and Culloden, was, on the night of Saturday, 20 February 1799, removed and carried forward into the sea about two hundred and sixty yards. The explanation seemed to be that ice eighteen inches thick round the stone had been raised by the tide, and the stone with it, during a hurricane.'

This stone may clearly be seen at low tide from Alturlie Point on the south side of Petty Bay.

The Seer was at one time in the Culloden district on some important business. While passing over what is now so well known as the Battlefield of Culloden, he exclaimed, 'Oh! Drummossie, thy bleak moor shall, ere many generations have passed away, be stained with the best blood of the Highlands. Glad am I that I will not see that day, for it will be a fearful period; heads will be lopped off by the score, and no mercy will be shown or quarter given on either side.' It is perhaps unnecessary to point out how literally this prophecy has been fulfilled on the occasion of the last battle fought on British soil. We have received several other versions of it from different parts of the country, almost all in identical terms.

There are several variations of the above prediction worth quoting.

'The day will come when the wheel at Millburn will be turned for three successive days with water red with human blood; for on the lade's bank a fierce battle shall be fought in which much blood will be spilt.'

Culloden Battlefield and Visitors' Centre is owned by the National Trust for Scotland. Every year thousands of visitors come to see the site where in April 1746 the Hanoverians under the Duke of Cumberland with a minimum loss of men slaughtered 2,000 Royalists under Prince Charles Edward Stuart. The battle marked the beginning of a deep decline in prosperity from which the Highlands have only recently begun to recover.

'There is a shadow over Culloden. That shadow covers Scotland but that shadow will rise and the sun will shine over Scotland brighter than it has done before.'

This was contributed by Mrs Higginbotham in a letter to the Scots Magazine in 1982. Some would claim that the prophecy has yet to be fulfilled and that the Highlands have not yet fully recovered from the disaster of Culloden.

'The time will come when whisky or dram shops will be so plentiful that one may be met with almost at the head of every plough furrow.' (*Thig an latha 's am bi tighean-oil cho lionmhor 's nach mor nach fhaicear tigh-osda aig ceann gach claise.*) 'Policemen will become so numerous in every town that they may be met with at the corner of every street.' 'Travelling merchants' [pedlars and hawkers] 'will be so plentiful that a person can scarcely walk a mile on the public highway without meeting one of them.'

The following is from *A Summer in Skye*, by the late Alex. Smith, author of *A Life Drama*. Describing Dunvegan Castle and its surroundings, he says: – 'Dun Kenneth's prophecy has come to pass – "In the days of Norman, son of the third Norman, there will be a noise in the doors of the people, and wailing in the house of the widow; and Macleod will not have so many gentlemen of his name as will row a five-oared boat round the Maidens." If the last trumpet had been sounded at the end of the French war, no one but a Macleod would have risen out of the churchyard of Dunvegan. If you want to see a chief (of the Macleods) nowadays you must go to London for him.' There can be no question as to these having been fulfilled to the letter.

Dunvegan is one of the best known castles in Scotland and is the seat of Clan Macleod. Situated on a sea-loch in north-west Skye, it seems to grow out of the rock above the shore. Its origins are lost in antiquity but it has been so much altered and remodelled that the oldest remaining part is the Fairy Tower which dates from the sixteenth century. Its history, however, dates back to Norse times when Leod, son of Olaf the Black, King of Man, acquired Dunvegan by marrying a Scandinavian princess; and their sons, Norman and Torquil, founded the Macleod branches in Harris and Lewis.

It was Ian, the fourth chief, who received the Fairy Flag, so it is said, when his infant son was found by his nurse mysteriously wrapped up in it. When she brought him to the great hall, voices were heard proclaiming that the banner was a fairy gift which would save the clan in three great dangers. William, the seventh chief, was killed at the Battle of Bloody Bay during James IV's campaign to subdue the Lordship of the Isles, and his son, Alastair Crookback, after sampling the sophistication of Edinburgh court life, entertained James V on the top of one of two mountains known as Macleods' Tables, surrounded by his clansmen holding torches. It was he who built the Fairy Tower and established the MacCrimmon school of pipers. Sir Rory Mor, sixteenth chief, was knighted by James VI and lived in kingly style surrounded by a court of gentlemen, harpers, bards and jesters. Norman, twenty-second chief, entertained Boswell and Johnson during their Hebridean trip.

When Skye was struck with famine in 1847, the chief ruined himself to support his people and had to move to London to find employment while many of the clan were forced to emigrate. The Macleods found a new unity under their late chief, Dame Flora Macleod of Macleod, who inherited Dunvegan in 1935 and who turned the castle into a world centre for her clan.

'The day will come when a fox will rear a litter of cubs on the hearthstone of Castle Downie.'

Castle Downie or Dounie was the Gaelic name for Beaufort, the seat of the Frasers of Lovat. The original castle was burned by the Hanoverians in 1746. The present Beaufort Castle was built in 1878 in the 'Field of Downie'. After the recent death of the 24th 'MacShimidh' (son of Simon) Chief of the Clan, 17th Lord Fraser of Lovat, and outstanding Commando leader in the Second World War, Beaufort Castle was sold to a businesswoman from Dundee who is a member of Clan Fraser.

'The day will come when a wild deer will be caught alive at Chanonry Point, in the Black Isle.' All these things have come to pass.

With respect to the clearances in Lewis, he said – 'Many a long waste *feannag* (rig, once arable) will yet be seen between Uig of the Mountains and Ness of the Plains.' That this prediction had been fulfilled to the letter, no one acquainted with the country will deny.

The following would appear to have been made solely on account of the unlikelihood of the occurrence: – 'A Lochalsh woman shall weep over the grave of a Frenchman in the burying-place of Lochalsh.' People imagined they could discern in this an allusion to some battle on the West Coast, in which French troops would be engaged; but there was an occurrence which gave it a very different interpretation. A native of Lochalsh married a French footman, who died, shortly after this event, and was interred in the burying-ground of Lochalsh, thus leaving his widow to mourn over his grave. This may appear a commonplace matter enough, but it must be remembered that a Frenchman in Lochalsh, and especially a Frenchman whom a Highland woman would mourn over, in Coinneach's day, was a very different phenomenon to what it is in our days of railways, tourists and steamboats.

The Seer also predicted the formation of a railway through the Muir of Ord, handed down in the following stanza:

Nuair a bhios de eaglais an Sgire na Toiseachd,
A's lamh da ordaig an I-Stian',
Da dhrochaid aig Sguideal nan geocaire,
As fear da imleag an Dunean,
Thig Miltearan a Carn a-chlarsair,
Air Carbad gun each gun srian,
A dh-fhagas am Blar-dubh na thasach,
'Dortadh fuil le iomadh sgian;
A's olaidh am fitheach a thri saitheachd
De dh-fhuil nan Gaidheal, bho clach nam Fionn.

Here is a literal translation:

When there shall be two churches in the Parish of Ferrintosh,
And a hand with two thumbs in *I-Stiana,*

Two bridges at *Sguideal* (Conon) of the gormandizers,
And a man with two navels at Dunean,
Soldiers will come from *Carn a Chlarsair* (Tarradale)
On a chariot without horse or bridle,
Which will leave the *Blar-dubh* (Muir of Ord) a wilderness,
Spilling blood with many knives;
And the raven shall drink his three fulls
Of the blood of the Gael from the Stone of Fionn.

We already have two churches in the Parish of Ferrintosh, two bridges at Conon, and we are told by an eye-witness that there is actually at this very time a man with two thumbs on each hand in *I-Stiana*, in the Black Isle, and a man in the neighbourhood of Dunean who has two navels. The 'chariot without horse or bridle' is undoubtedly the 'iron horse'. What particular event the latter part of the prediction refers to, it is impossible to say; but if we are to have any faith in the Seer, something serious is looming not very remotely in the future.

Mr Macintyre supplies the following, which is clearly a fragment of the one above given: – Coinneach Odhar foresaw the formation of a railway through the Muir of Ord which he said 'would be a sign of calamitous times'. The prophecy regarding this is handed down to us in the following form: – 'I would not like to live when a black bridleless horse shall pass through the Muir of Ord.'

Some local tradition holds that this prediction was fulfilled when the Duke of Portland – before the days of the railway in the north – travelled by a road car driven by steam.

Fearchair a Ghunna. (Farquhar of the Gun, an idiotic simpleton who lived during the latter part of his extraordinary life on the Muir of Tarradale) seems, in his own quaint way, to have entered into the spirit of this prophecy, when he compared the train, as it first passed through the district, to the funeral of 'Old Nick'.

Farquhar Maclennan, known as the Ross-shire Wanderer, was well-known to laird and crofter alike, in the parish of Killearnan in the Black Isle, as a 'gentleman of the road'. Born in Strathconon in 1784 of crofter parents, he was employed as herdsboy to a Ferrintosh farmer who, in a fit of not wholly unjustified anger, struck the lad over the head with a spade – which was, no doubt, the cause of his eccentricity. He gave up regular employment and took to the roads. The old tramp was as odd in appearance as he was original in conversation. He wore an ancient wideawake hat stuck all over with feathers and pieces of paper and secured under his chin with an iron chain. A second and heavier chain was tied round his brightly coloured clothes, to which were attached pieces of metal, rags, bones, pistols and a Mexican powder-horn, among other things. His main diet consisted of crows. He had a passion for stones which he would blast with gunpowder given him on the sly by friendly keepers; but dearest of all his possessions was his gun, a fearful contraption consisting of half a dozen old gun barrels tied together to resemble a revolver, the stock of which he had made from a tree trunk. Apart from his witticisms which consisted mainly of getting the better of local ministers, his claim to fame and respect rested in his famous prayer, as personal and touching a tribute as was ever heard at kitchen hearth or woodland fire, as may be judged from the following short excerpt:

'O Blessed Trinity, thou art here now and east at Tain. Thou art giving slated houses to the big folk, but thou hast given a black sooty bothy which won't keep out the rain from Fearchair's body to me. . . . Bless the bones, feathers, rags, keys and iron. Bless also the wood, hemp, cotton, tea and sugar, though poor Fearchair's share of them be small. . . . Bless everything, O Blessed Trinity, for thou has created all.'

He died aged eighty-four, after a day at his favourite occupation, blasting stones; and was buried at Tomnahurich Cemetery, Inverness.

Tradition gives another version, viz: – 'that after four successive dry summers, a fiery chariot shall pass through the *Blar-dubh*', which has been very literally fulfilled. Coinneach Odhar was not the only person that had a view beforehand of this railyway line, for it is commonly reported that a man residing in the neighbourhood of Beauly, gifted with second sight, had a vision of the train, moving along in all its headlong speed, when he was on his way home one dark autumn night, several years before the question of forming a railway in those parts was mooted.

Here are two other Gaelic stanzas having undoubted reference to the Mackenzies of Rosehaugh.

Rosehaugh in the Black Isle was given its name by Sir George Mackenzie of Avoch, Lord-Advocate for Scotland in the second half of the seventeenth century, because of the profusion of wild roses that grew there. He was succeeded by his third son, who had a daughter who was to die without issue, thus ending that particular branch of the clan.

Bheir Tanaistear Chlann Choinnich
Rocus bàn ás a choille;
'S bheir e ceile bho tigh-ciuil
Le a mhuinntir 'na aghaidh;
'S gum bi' n Tanaistear mor
Ann an gniomh 's an ceann-labhairt,
'Nuair bhios am Pap' anns an Roimh
Air a thilgeadh dheth chathair,
Thall fa chomhar Creàg-a-Chodh
Comhnuichidh taillear caol odhar;
'S Seumas gorach mar thighearn,
'S Seumas glic mar fhear tomhais –
A mharcaicheas gun srian
Air loth fhiadhaich a roghainn;
Ach cuiridh mor-chuis gun chiall
'N aite siol nam fiadh siol nan gobhar;
'S tuitidh an t-Eilean-dubh briagha
Fuidh riaghladh iasgairean Auch.

Literal translation:

The heir (or chief) of the Mackenzies will take
A white rook out of the wood,

And will take a wife from a music house (dancing saloon),
With his people against him!
And the heir will be great
In deeds and as an orator,
When the Pope in Rome
Will be thrown off his throne.

Over opposite Creag-a-Chow
Will dwell a diminutive lean tailor,
Also Foolish James as the laird,
And Wise James as a measurer,
Who will ride without a bridle
The wild colt of his choice;
But foolish pride without sense
Will put in the place of the seed of the deer the seed of the goat;
And the beautiful Black Isle will fall
Under the management of the fishermen of Avoch.

We have not learnt that any of the Rosehaugh Mackenzies has yet
taken a *white* rook from the woods; nor have we heard anything
suggested as to what this part of the prophecy may refer to. We
are, however, credibly informed that one of the late Mackenzies
of Rosehaugh had taken his wife from a music saloon in one of
our southern cities, and that his people were very much against
him for so doing. One of them, Sir George, no doubt was 'great
in deeds and as an orator', but we fail to discover any connection
between the time in which he lived and the time 'when the Pope
in Rome will be thrown off his throne'. We were unable in the
first edition to suggest the meaning of the first six lines of the last
stanza, but Mr Maclennan supplies us with the following explanation: – 'I have been hearing these lines discussed since I was a boy,
and being a native of Rosehaugh, I took a special interest in everything concerning it. The first two lines I was repeatedly informed,
referred to a pious man who lived on the estate of Bennetsfield,
opposite Craigiehow, when *Seumas Gorach* (Foolish James referred to in the third line), was proprietor of Rosehaugh. This

godly man, who was contemporary with Foolish James, often warned him of his end, and predicted his fate if he did not mend his ways; and as he thus *cut* his bounds for him, he is supposed to be the "diminutive lean tailor". He is still in life. We all knew "Foolish James". The fourth line refers to James Maclaren, who lived at Rosehaugh most of the time during which the last two Mackenzies ruled over it and only died two years ago. He was an odd character, but a very straightforward man; often rebuked "Foolish James" for the reckless and fearless manner in which he rode about, and set bounds before the "foolish" laird, which he was not allowed to pass. Maclaren was, on that account, believed to be the "measurer" referred to by the Seer. The fifth and sixth lines are supposed to apply to the wife fancied by Mackenzie in a "dancing saloon", who was always considered the "wild colt", at whose instigation he rode so recklessly and foolishly.' We wish the realizations of our prophet's predictions in this case were a little less fanciful.

Those in the seventh and eighth lines have been most literally fulfilled, for there can be no doubt that 'foolish pride without sense' has brought about what the Seer predicted, and secured, for the present at least, the seed of the goat where the seed of the deer used to rule. The deer, and the deer's horns, as is well known, are the armorial bearings of the Mackenzies, while the goat is that of the Fletchers, who now rule in Rosehaugh, on the ruins of its once great and famous *Cabarfeidh*.

Part of the beautiful Black Isle has already fallen under the management of the son of a fisherman of Avoch; and who knows but other fishermen from that humble village may yet amass sufficient wealth to buy the whole. The old proprietors, we regret, are rapidly making way with their 'foolish pride without sense', for someone to purchase it.

We are informed that the present proprietor of Rosehaugh is the son of an Avoch fisherman – the son of a Mr Jack, who followed that honourable avocation in this humble village for many years; afterwards left the place and went to reside in Elgin, where he commenced business as a small general dealer, or 'huckster';

that some of the boys – his sons – exhibited a peculiar smartness while in school; that this was noticed by a lady relative of their mother, an aunt, of the name of Fletcher, who encouraged and helped on the education of the boys, and who took one or more of them to her own home, and brought them up; afterwards they found their way south, and ultimately became successful merchants and landed proprietors. (In corroboration of the main facts here stated, we quote the following from *Walford's County Families of the United Kingdom*: – 'Fletcher, James, Esq. of Rosehaugh, Ross-shire, son of the late Wm. Jack, Esq., by Isabel, dau. of the late Charles Fletcher, Esq., and brother of J. C. Fletcher, Esq ; b. 18—; m. 1852, Frederica Mary, dau. of John Stephen, Esq., niece of Sir Alfred Stephen, C.B., Chief Justice of New South Wales, and widow of Alexander Hay, Esq., of the 58th Regt. . . . He assumed the name of Fletcher in lieu of his patronymic on the death of his mother in 1856.')

James Fletcher bought the estate of Rosehaugh in the Black Isle in 1864 for £145,000. Between 1895 and 1902 his son and heir, James Douglas Fletcher, a brilliant financier, converted the original house into a large mansion built in the ornate style of a Renaissance chateau designed by the architect William Flockhart. The Fletchers were responsible for adding many Black Isle properties to the original estate and for providing employment for the Avoch villagers. At the death of Mrs Fletcher in 1953, the estate was sold and because no one could be found to buy it, the mansion was demolished in 1959. In further fulfilment of the prophecy, every Avoch fishermen now owns his own cottage.

These are facts of which we were entirely ignorant when first writing down the stanzas already given. The verses were sent to us from various quarters, and they have undoubtedly been floating about the country for generations. So much for the Seer's prophetic power in this instance. Were we better acquainted with the history of the other families referred to in the stanzas, it is probable that more light could be thrown upon what they refer to than we are at present able to do.

While we are dealing with the 'wonderful' in connection with

the House of Rosehaugh, it may not be out of place to give a few
instances of the somewhat extraordinary experiences of the famous
Sir George Mackenzie of Rosehaugh already referred to. He was
one of the most distinguished members of the Scottish Bar, was
Lord-Advocate for Scotland in the reign of Charles the Second,
and was, indeed, a contemporary of the Brahan Seer. His 'Insti-
tutes' are still considered a standing authority by the legal profession: – On one occasion, while at Rosehaugh, a poor widow
from a neighbouring estate called to consult him regarding her
being repeatedly warned to remove from a small croft which she
held under a lease of several years, but as some time had yet to run
before its expiry, and being threatened with summary ejection
from the croft, she went to solicit his advice. Having examined the
tenor of the lease, Sir George informed her that it contained a
flaw, which, in case of opposition, would render her success ex-
ceedingly doubtful; and although it was certainly an oppressive
act to deprive her of her croft, he thought her best plan was to
submit. However, seeing the distressed state of mind in which the
poor woman was on hearing his opinion, he desired her to call
upon him the following day, when he would consider her case
more carefully. His clerk, who always slept in the same room as
his lordship, was not a little surprised, about midnight, to discover
him rising from his bed fast asleep, lighting a candle which stood
on his table, drawing in his chair, and commencing to write very
busily, as if he had been all the time wide awake. The clerk saw
how he was employed, but he never spoke a word, and, when he
had finished, he saw him place what he had written in his private
desk, locking it, extinguishing the candle, and then retiring to bed
as if nothing had happened. Next morning at breakfast, Sir George
remarked that he had had a very strange dream about the poor
widow's threatened ejectment, which, he could now remember,
and he had now no doubt of making out a clear case in her favour.
His clerk rose from the table, asked for the key of his desk, and
brought therefrom several pages of manuscript; and, as he handed
them to Sir George, enquired – 'Is that like your dream?' On looking over it for a few seconds, Sir George said, 'Dear me, this is

singular; this is my very dream!' He was no less surprised when his clerk informed him of the manner in which he had acted; and, sending for the widow, he told her what steps to adopt to frustrate the efforts of her oppressors. Acting on the counsel thus given, the poor widow was ultimately successful, and, with her young family, was allowed to remain in possession of her 'wee bit croftie' without molestation.

Sir George principally resided at this time in Edinburgh, and, before dinner, invariably walked for half an hour. The place he selected for this was Leith Walk, then almost a solitary place. One day, while taking his accustomed exercise, he was met by a venerable-looking, grey-headed old gentleman, who accosted him and, without introduction or apology, said – 'There is a very important case to come off in London fourteen days hence, at which your presence will be required. It is a case of heirship to a very extensive estate in the neighourhood of London, and a pretended claimant is doing his utmost to disinherit the real heir, on the ground of his inability to produce proper titles thereto. It is necessary that you be there on the day mentioned; and in one of the attics of the mansion-house on the estate there is an old oak chest with two bottoms; between these you will find the necessary titles, written on parchment.' Having given this information, the old man disappeared, leaving Sir George quite bewildered; but the latter, resuming his walk, soon recovered his previous equanimity, and thought nothing further of the matter.

Next day, while taking his walk in the same place, he was again met by the same old gentleman, who earnestly urged him not to delay by another day in repairing to London, assuring him that he would be handsomely rewarded for his trouble; but to this Sir George paid no particular attention. The third day he was again met by the same hoary-headed sire, who energetically pleaded with him not to lose a day in setting out, otherwise the case would be lost. His singular deportment, and his anxiety that Sir George should be present at the discussion of the case, in which he seemed so deeply interested, induced Sir George to give in to his earnest importunities, and accordingly he started next morning on horseback, arriving in London on the day preceding that on which the case was to come on. In a few hours he was pacing in front of the mansion-house described by the old man at Leith Walk, where he met two gentlemen engaged in earnest conversation – one of the claimants to the property, and a celebrated London barrister – to whom he immediately introduced himself as the principal law-officer of the Crown for Scotland. The barrister, no doubt supposing that Sir George was coming to take the bread out of his mouth, addressed him in a surly manner, and spoke disrespectfully of his country; to which the latter replied, 'that, lame and ignorant as his learned friend took the Scotch to be, yet in law, as well as in other respects, they would effect what would defy him and all his London clique'. This disagreeable dialogue was put an end to by the other gentleman – the claimant to the property – taking Sir George into the house. After sitting and conversing for some minutes, Sir George expressed a wish to be shown over the house. The drawing-room was hung all round with magnificent pictures and drawings, which Sir George greatly admired; but there was one which particularly attracted his attention; and after examining it very minutely, he, with a surprised expression, inquired of his conductor whose picture it was? and received the answer – 'It is my great-great-grandfather's.' 'My goodness!' exclaimed Sir George, 'the very man who spoke to me three times on three successive days in Leith Walk, and at whose urgent request I came here!' Sir George, at his own request, was then conducted to the attics, in one of which there was a large mass of old papers, which was turned up and examined without discovering anything to assist them in prosecuting the claim to the heirship of the property. However, as they were about giving up the search, Sir George noticed an old trunk lying in a corner, which, his companion told him, had lain there for many a year as lumber, and contained nothing. The Leith Walk gentleman's information recurring to Sir George, he gave the old moth-eaten chest a good hearty kick, such as could wish to have been received by his 'learned friend' the barrister, who spoke so disrespectfully of his country. The bottom flew out of the trunk, with a quantity of chaff, among which the original titles to the property were discovered. Next morning Sir George entered the court just as the case was about to be called and addressed the pretended claimant's counsel – 'Well, sir, what shall I offer you to abandon this action?' 'No sum, or any consideration whatever, would induce me to give it up,' answered his learned opponent. 'Well, sir,' said Sir George, at the same time pulling out his snuff-horn and taking a pinch, 'I will not even hazard a pinch on it.' The case was called. Sir George, in reply to the claimant's counsel, in an eloquent speech, addressed the bench; exposed most effectually the means which had been adopted to deprive his client of his birthright; concluded by producing the titles found in the old chest; and the case was at once decided in favour of his client. The decision being announced, Sir George took the young heir's arm, and, bowing to his learned friend the barrister, remarked, 'You see now what a Scotsman has done, and let me tell you that I wish a countryman of mine anything but a London barrister.' Sir George immediately returned to Edinburgh, well paid for his trouble; but he never again, in his favourite walk, encountered the old grey-headed gentleman.

The following two stanzas refer to the Mackenzies of Kilcoy and their property:

Nuair a ghlaodhas paisdean tigh Chulchallaidh,
'Tha slige ar mortairean dol thairis!'
Thig bho Chròidh madadh ruadh
Bhi's 'measg an t-sluaigh mar mhadadh-alluidh,
Rè da-fhichead biadhna a's corr,
'S gum bi na chòta iomadh mallachd;
'N sin tilgear e gu falamh brònach
Mar shean sguab air cùl an doruis;
A's bithidh an tuath mhor mar eunlaith sporsail,
'S an tighearnan cho bochd ris na sporais –
Tha beannachd 'san onair bhoidhich,
A's mallachd an dortadh na fola.

Nuair bhitheas caisteal ciar Chulchallaidh
Na sheasaidh fuar, agus falamh,
'S na cathagan 's na rocuis
Gu seolta sgiathail thairis,
Gabhaidh duine graineal comhnuidh,
Ri thaobh, mi-bheusal a's salach,
Nach gleidh guidhe stal-phosaidh,
'S nach eisd ri cleireach no caraid,
Ach bho Chreag-a-chodh gu Sgire na Toiseachd
Gum bi muisean air toir gach caileag –
A's ochan! ochan! s' ma leon,
Sluigidh am balgaire suas moran talamh!

Literally translated:

When the girls of Kilcoy house cry out,
'The shell (cup) of our murders is flowing over.'
A fox from Croy will come
Who shall be like a wolf among the people
During forty years and more,
And in his coat shall be many curses;
He shall then be thrown empty and sorrowful,
Like an old besom behind the door;
The large farmers will be like sportful birds,
And the lairds as poor as the sparrows –
There's a blessing in handsome honesty
And curses in the shedding of blood.

When the stern Castle of Kilcoy
Shall stand cold and empty,
And the jackdaws and the rooks
Are artfully flying past it,
A loathsome man shall then dwell
Beside it, indecent and filthy,
Who will not keep the vow of the marriage coif,
Listen neither to cleric nor friend;

But from Creag-a-Chow to Ferrintosh
The dirty fellow will be after every girl –
Ochan! Ochan!! woe's me,
The cunning dog will swallow up much land.

Built in the early seventeenth century, Kilcoy Castle was one in a line of defensive sites owned by the all-powerful Mackenzies. In 1618, Alexander Mackenzie, known as Alexander the Knife, possessed a chart for the land. He must have lived to a good age, for it was he who carved the handsome lintel over the fireplace in the hall which is dated 1679. The Mackenzies possessed Kilcoy for nearly three hundred years, though the last to live there died in 1813, when the castle fell into a ruinous state; but in this instance the Seer did not see far enough, for Kilcoy has been fully restored into a very fine private property.

The history of the Kilcoy family has been an unfortunate one in late years, and the second and last lines of the first stanza clearly refer to a well-known tragic incident in the recent history of this once highly-favoured and popular Highland family.

Mr Maclennan applies them to an earlier event, and says: 'The second and last line of the first stanza refer to the following story – Towards the latter end of the seventeenth century a large number of cattle, in the Black Isle, were attacked with a strange malady, which invariably ended in madness and in death. The disease was particularly destructive on the Kilcoy and Redcastle estates, and the proprietors offered a large sum of money as a reward to any who should find a remedy. An old warlock belonging to the parish agreed to protect the cattle from the ravages of this unknown disease, for the sum offered, if they provided him with a human sacrifice. To this ghastly proposal the lairds agreed. A large barn at Parkton was, from its secluded position, selected as a suitable place for the horrid crime, where a poor friendless man, who lived at Linwood, close to the site of the present Free Church manse, was requested, under some pretence, to appear on a certain day. The unsuspecting creature obeyed the summons of his superiors; he was instantly bound and disembowelled alive by the horrid wizard, who dried the heart, liver, kidneys, pancreas, and reduced them to powder, of which he ordered a little to be given to the diseased animals in water. Before the unfortunate victim breathed his last, he ejaculated the following imprecation: *Gum b' ann nach tig an latha 'bhitheas teaghlach a Chaisteil Ruaidh gun oinseach, na teaglach Chulchallaidh gun amadan.* (Let the day never come when the family of Redcastle shall be without a female idiot, or the family of Kilcoy without a fool.) It appears, not only that this wild imprecation was to some extent realized, but also that the Brahan Seer, years before, knew and predicted that it would be made, and that its prayer would be ultimately granted.'

Unlike Kilcoy Castle which is situated about a mile north, Redcastle belongs to a much older period and has had a long and bloody history. Originally called Eddydor (Between the Waters) it was built by David, brother of William the Lyon, in 1179, at the same time as Dunskaith at Nigg Bay. It belonged in 1230 to Sir John Bisset, whose daughter brought Beauly to the Frasers as her dowry, and after a period of violence was annexed to the Crown by James II. By 1492 it had been seized by the Mackenzies, and after much rowing and raiding it remained a Mackenzie stronghold until 1790, when the laird was cheated out of it for £25,000. By 1824 the price of Highland land had risen so high, due to the exchange of crofters for sheep, that it was resold to Sir William Fettes for £135,000. It finally came into the hands of the Baillies of Dochfour and was last occupied by the army during the Second World War. Since then it has become a roofless ruin. It is said to be haunted by the ghost of a child buried under the cornerstone, an ancient rite to ward off evil spirits.

Who the 'fox from Croy' is, we are at present unable to suggest; but taking the two stanzas as they stand, it would be difficult to describe the position of the family and the state of the castle, with our present knowledge of their history, and in their present position, more faithfully than Coinneach Odhar has done more than two centuries ago. What a faithful picture of the respective positions of the great farmers and the lairds of the present day! And what a contrast between their relative positions now and at the time when the Seer predicted the change!

In the appendix to the *Life of the late Dr Norman Macleod*, by his brother, the Rev Donald Macleod, DD, a series of autobiographical reminiscences are given, which the famous Rev Norman, the Doctor's father, dictated in his old age to one of his daughters. In the summer of 1799 he visited Dunvegan Castle, the stronghold of the Macleods, in the Isle of Skye. Those of the prophecies already given in verse are, undoubtedly, fragments of the long rhythmical productions of Coinneach Odhar Fiosaiche's prophecies regarding most of our Highland families, to which the Rev Norman refers, and of which the prophecy given in his reminiscences is as follows:

'One circumstance took place at the Castle (Dunvegan) on this occasion which I think worth recording, especially as I am the only person now living who can attest the truth of it. There had been a traditionary prophecy, couched in Galic verse, regarding the family of Macleod, which on this occasion, received a most extraordinary fulfilment. This prophecy I have heard repeated by several persons, and most deeply do I regret that I did not take a copy of it when I could have got it. The worthy Mr Campbell of Knock, in Mull, had a very beautiful version of it, as also had my father, and so, I think, had likewise Dr Campbell of Killinver. Such prophecies were current regarding almost all old families in the Highlands; the Argyll family were of the number; and there is a prophecy regarding the Breadalbane family as yet unfulfilled which I hope may remain so. The present Marquis of Breadalbane is fully aware of it, as are many of the connections of the family. Of the Macleod family, it was prophesied at least a hundred years prior to the circumstance which I am about to relate.

'In the prophecy to which I am about to allude, it was foretold that when Norman, the Third Norman (*Tormadnan'tri Tormaid*), the son of the hard-boned English lady (*Mac na mnatha caoile cruaidhe Shassunaich*) would perish by an accidental death; that when the "Maidens" of Macleod (certain well-known rocks on the coast of Macleod's country) became the property of a Campbell; when a fox had young ones in one of the turrets of the Castle, and particularly when the Fairy enchanted banner should be for the last time exhibited, then the glory of the Macleod family should depart; a great part of the estate should be sold to others; so that a small "curragh", a boat, would carry all gentlemen of the name of Macleod across Loch Dunvegan; but that in times far distant another John Breac should arise, who should redeem those estates, and raise the power and honours of the house to a higher pitch than ever. Such in general terms was the prophecy. And now as to the curious coincidence of its fulfilment.

'There was, at this time, at Dunvegan, an English smith, with whom I became a favourite, and who told me, in solemn secrecy, that the iron chest which contained the "fairy flag" was to be forced open next morning; that he had arranged with Mr Hector Macdonald Buchanan to be there with his tools for that purpose.

'I was most anxious to be present, and I asked permission to that effect of Mr Buchanan (Macleod's man of business), who granted me leave on condition that I should not inform anyone of the name of Macleod that such was intended, and should keep it a profound secret from the chief. This I promised and most faithfully acted on. Next morning we proceeded to the chamber in the East Turret, where was the iron chest that contained the famous flag, about which there is an interesting tradition.

'With great violence the smith tore open the lid of this iron chest; but, in doing so, a key was found under part of the covering, which would have opened the chest, had it been found in time. There was an inner case, in which we found the flag, enclosed in a wooden box of strongly scented wood. The flag consisted of a square piece of very rich silk, with crosses wrought with gold thread, and several elf-spots stitched with great care on different parts of it.

'On this occasion, the melancholy news of the death of the young and promising heir of Macleod reached the Castle. "Norman, the third Norman", was a lieutenant of HMS, the *Queen Charlotte*, which was blown up at sea, and he and the rest perished. At the same time, the rocks called "Macleod's Maidens" were sold, in the course of that very week, to Angus Campbell of Ensay, and they are still in possession of his grandson. A fox in possession of a Lieutenant Maclean, residing in the West Turret of the Castle, had young ones, which I handled, and thus all that was said in the prophecy alluded to was so far fulfilled, although I am glad the family of my chief still enjoy their ancestral possessions, and the worst part of the prophecy accordingly remains unverified. I merely state the facts of the case as they occurred, without expressing any opinion whatever as to the nature of these traditionary legends with which they were connected.'

The estates are still, we are glad to say, in possession of the ancient family of Macleod, and the present chief is rapidly improving the prospects of his house. The probabilities are therefore at present against our prophet. The hold of the Macleods on their estates is getting stronger instead of weaker, and the John Breac who is to be the future deliverer has not only not yet appeared, but the undesirable position of affairs requiring his services is yet, we hope, in the distant future.

The Seer predicted that 'when the big-thumbed Sheriff Officer and the bland [man] of the twenty-four fingers shall be together in Barra, Macneil of Barra may be making ready for the flitting'. (*Nuair a bhitheas maor nan ordagan mora agus dall nan ceithir-meoraibh-fichead comhla ann am Barraidh, faodaidh MacNeill Bharraidh 'bhi deanamh deiseil na h-imirich.*) This prediction, which was known in Barra for generations, has been most literally fulfilled. On a certain occasion, 'the blind of the twenty-four fingers', so called from having six fingers on each hand, and six toes on each foot, left Benbecula on a tour, to collect alms in South Barra before returning home. Arriving at the Ferry – the isthmus which separates South Uist from Barra – he met *Maor nan Ordagan mora*, and they crossed the kyle in the same boat. It was afterwards found that the officer was actually on his way to serve a summons of ejectment on the laird of Barra; and poor Macneil not only had to make ready for, but had indeed to make the flitting. The man who had acted as guide to the blind on the occasion is, we are informed, still living and in excellent health, though considerably over eighty years of age.

Clan MacNeil claims descent from Neil of the Nine Hostages, High King of Ireland in AD 397, in the person of Neil of the Castle, who is alleged to have built the beautiful and romantic castle of Kisimul in 1030. Situated in Castle-bay on the Isle of Barra, it was the seat of the MacNeils until 1838 when General MacNeil, the fortieth chief, was forced to sell owing to the failure of the kelp industry. Kisimul was left deserted until 1937 when the forty-fifth chief, Robert Lister MacNeil, an American citizen, fulfilled his lifelong dream of restoring the castle and making it his home.

The following is said to have been fulfilled by the conduct of the Duke of Cumberland at and after the battle of Culloden. The Seer was, on one occasion, passing Millburn, on his way from Inverness to Petty, and noticing the old mill, which was a very primitive building, thatched with divots, he said: 'The day will come when thy wheel shall be turned for three successive days by water red with human blood; for on the banks of thy lade a fierce battle shall be fought, at which much blood shall be spilt.' Some say that this is as yet unfulfilled; and it has been suggested that the battle may yet be fought in connection with the Barracks now building at the Hut of Health.

Coinneach also prophecied remarkable things regarding the Mackenzies of Fairburn and Fairburn Tower. 'The day will come when the Mackenzies of Fairburn shall lose their entire possessions, and that branch of the clan shall disappear almost to a man from the face of the earth. Their Castle shall become uninhabited, desolate, and forsaken, and a cow shall give birth to a calf in the uppermost chamber in Fairburn Tower.' The first part of this prophecy has only too literally come to pass; and within the memory of hundreds now living, and who knew Coinneach's prophecy years before it was fulfilled, the latter part – that referring to the cow calving in the uppermost chamber – has also been undoubtedly realized. We are personally acquainted with people whose veracity is beyond question, who knew the prophecy, and who actually took the trouble at the time to go all the way from Inverness to see the cow-mother and her offspring in the Tower, before they were taken down. Mr Maclennan supplies the following version: – Coinneach said, addressing a large concourse of people – 'Strange as it may appear to all those who may hear me this day, yet what I am about to tell you is true and will come to pass at the appointed time. The day will come when a cow shall give birth to a calf in the uppermost chamber (*seomar uachdarach*) of Fairburn Castle. The child now unborn will see it.'

When the Seer uttered this prediction, the Castle of Fairburn was in the possession of, and occupied by, a very rich and powerful chieftain, to whom homage was paid by many of the neighbouring lairds. Its halls rang loud with sounds of music and of mirth, and happiness reigned within its portals. On its winding stone stairs trod and passed carelessly to and fro pages and liveried servants in their wigs and golden trimmings. Nothing in the world was more unlikely to happen, to all appearance, than what the Seer predicted, and Coinneach was universally ridiculed for having given utterance to what was apparently so nonsensical; but this abuse and ridicule the Seer bore with the patient self-satisfied air of one who was fully convinced of the truth of what he uttered. Years passed by, but no sign of the fulfilment of the prophecy. The Seer, the Laird of Fairburn, and the whole of that generation were gathered to their fathers, and still no signs of the curious prediction being realized. The Laird of Fairburn's immediate successors also followed their predecessors, and the Seer, to all appearance, was fast losing his reputation as a prophet. The tower was latterly left uninhabited, and it soon fell into a dilapidated state of repair – its doors decayed and fell away from their hinges, one by one, until at last there was no door on the main stair from the floor to the roof. Some years after, and not long ago, the Fairburn tenant-farmer stored away some straw in the uppermost chamber of the tower; in the process, some of the straw dropped, and was left strewn on the staircase. One of his cows on a certain day chanced to find her way to the main door of the tower, and finding it open, began to pick up the straw scattered along the stair. The animal proceeded thus, till she had actually arrived at the uppermost chamber, whence, being heavy in calf, she was unable to descend. She was consequently left in the tower until she gave birth to a fine healthy calf. They were allowed to remain there for several days, where many went to see them, after which the cow and her progeny were brought down; and Coinneach Odhar's prophecy was thus fulfilled to the letter.

Fairburn Tower stands high on a ridge between the Orrin and Conon valleys about five miles from Muir of Ord, and dates from the sixteenth century. Though badly ruined, it is still possible to see that the interior was once well appointed, with arched window recesses, moulded fireplaces and many aumbries. It rises for four stories with a garret under crow-stepped gables. During the mid-seventeenth century it was the property of Roderick Mackenzie, fifth laird of Fairburn, who was one of the richest and most respected chiefs in Ross-shire at the time. The line ended with Major-General Sir Alexander Mackenzie who died unmarried in 1850. The castle had been left to ruin for some time previous to this and by 1851, when the cow calved in the garret, it was being used by a local farmer to store hay. The prophecy was so well known that special transport was laid on from Inverness to Muir of Ord to enable curious sightseers to witness the fulfilment of the prediction for themselves.

A variation of the above prediction states that 'the day will come when a sow will litter in my lady's chamber at Fairburn Tower'. In 1827 Sir Roderick Murchieson of Tarradale in the Black Isle, President of the Geological and Geographical Societies, with a friend, decided to visit the tower which had been his mother's home. Later he wrote, 'We were groping our way up the broken staircase when we were almost knocked off our feet by the rush of two or three pigs that had been nestling upstairs in the very room in which my mother was born.' Sir Alexander Geikie, Sir Roderick's biographer, mentions that he knew the prophecy.

'The day will come when the Lewsmen shall go forth with their hosts to battle, but they will be turned back by the jaw-bone of an animal smaller than an ass,' was a prediction accounted ridiculous and quite incomprehensible until it was fulfilled in a remarkable but very simple manner. Seaforth and the leading men of the Clan, as is well known, were 'out in the '15 and '19', and had their estates forfeited; and it was only a few years before the '45 that their lands were again restored to Seaforth, and to Mackenzie, eleventh Baron of Hilton. The Rev Colin Mackenzie, a brother of Hilton, minister of Fodderty and Laird of Glack, in Aberdeenshire, was the first in the neighbourhood of Brahan who received information of Prince Charlie's landing in 1745. Seaforth had still a warm feeling for the Prince. His reverend friend, though a thorough Jacobite himself, was an intimate friend of Lord President Forbes, with whom he kept up a regular correspondence. He decided, no doubt mainly through his influence, to remain neutral himself, and fearing that his friend of Brahan might be led to join the Prince, he instantly, in receipt of the news, started for Brahan Castle. Although it was very late at night when he received the information, he crossed Knockfarrel, entered Seaforth's bedroom by the window – for he had already gone to rest for the night – and without awakening his lady, informed him of the landing of Charles. They decided upon getting out of the way, and both immediately disappeared. Seaforth was well known to have had previous correspondence with the Prince, and to have sent private orders to the Lews to have his men there in readiness; and Fodderty impressed upon him the prudence of getting out of sight altogether in the meantime. They started through the mountains in the direction of Poolewe, and some time afterwards, when there together in concealment near the shore, they saw two ships entering the bay, having on board a large number of armed men whom they at once recognized as Seaforth's followers from the Lews, raised and commanded by Captain Colin Mackenzie, the great-grandfather of Major Thomas Mackenzie of the 78th Highlanders. Lord Seaforth had just been making a repast of a sheep's head, when he espied his retainers, and approaching the ships with the sheep's jawbone in his hand, he waved it towards them, and ordered them to return to their homes at once, which command they obeyed by making at once for Stornoway; and thus was fulfilled Coinneach Odhar's apparently ludicrous prediction, that the brave Lewsmen would be turned back from battle with the jawbone of an animal smaller than an ass.

Mr Maclennan supplies us also with the following: – 'In the parish of Avoch is a well of beautiful clear water, out of which the Brahan Seer, upon one occasion, took a refreshing draught. So pleased was he with the water, that he looked at his Blue Stone, and said – "Whoever he be that drinketh of thy water henceforth, if suffering from any disease, shall, by placing two pieces of straw or wood on thy surface, ascertain whether he will recover or not. If he is to recover, the straws will whirl round in opposite directions; if he is to die soon, they will remain stationary." The writer (continued Mr Maclennan) knew people who went to the well and made the experiment. He was himself once unwell, and supposed to be at the point of death; he got of the water of the well, and he still lives. Whether it did him good or not, it is impossible to say, but this he does know, that the water pleased him uncommonly well.'

Although the parish of Avoch was well provided with springs, this prophecy is generally thought to refer to the Craiguck (now known as Craigie) Well, dedicated to St Bennet and situated on the north shore of Munlochy Bay in the old estate of Bennetsfield on the Black Isle. It dates back to pre-Christian days and, like the Cloutie Well at Munlochy dedicated to St Boniface, owes its supersitions to a much older pagan deity. It is still visited by local people on the first Sunday in May, who, if the ritual is to be correctly observed should spill a little of the water three times on the ground, cross themselves and fix a small offering of lace or silk to one of the overhanging trees as a gift to the guardian fairy of the well, before drinking and making a wish. Thus all deities are appeased! The better known Cloutie Well at Munlochy draws tourists from all over the world, and there are generations of rotting rags, ranging from car dusters to cardigans, attached to the tree and fence above the water. Many local inhabitants have been heard to say that they would like to get rid of the eyesore, but as tradition also decrees that any person unwise enough to remove a rag will inherit the misfortunes of the original owner, so far no one has dared.

With reference to Lady Hill, in the same parish, the Seer said – 'Thy name has gone far and wide; but though thy owners were brave on the field of battle, they never decked thy brow. The day will come, however, when a white collar shall be put upon thee. The child that is unborn shall see it, but I shall not.' This prediction has been fulfilled a few years ago, by the construction of a fine drive right round the hill.

Sometimes known as Ormond Hill, the castle of that name gave the style of Marquis to the Royal House of Stuart, and the last to bear the title was Charles I who was created Duke of Albany, Marquis of Ormond and Earl of Ross. Ormond Castle belong to the Moray (de Moravia) family during the 13th and 14th centuries. In 1297 during the Wars of Independence, while the surrounding strongholds of Dingwall, Cromarty, Inverness, Urquhart and Nairn were held by the English, Ormond Castle in Avoch and Balconie Castle in Easter Ross were held by the patriotic Scots for William Wallace by Sir Andrew de Moray. He fought bravely at the Battle of Stirling Bridge and died soon after, presumably from his wounds. His posthumous son, another Sir Andrew de Moray, married the sister of Robert Bruce and served as regent and guardian to the boy King David II. He was known as 'a lord of great beauty, sober and chaste-like, wise and stout, hardy and of great courage'. He ended his days at Ormond Castle and was buried in 1338 at 'the Cathedral Kirk of Rosmarkyn'. The castle was demolished by Cromwell's men and the stones used to build a citadel at Inverness. In May 1997, the 600th anniversary of raising the standard for Scotland's freedom was celebrated in style by the villagers of Avoch.

The road that was constructed round the hill during the last century was a popular drive for Victorian women on a Sunday afternoon. It survives only as a forestry track and the place where the castle once stood is partially overgrown with trees.

The Seer said, speaking of Beauly – 'The day will come, however distant, when Cnoc na Rath will be in the centre of the village.' It certainly would appear incredible, and even absurd, to suggest such a thing in Coinneach's day, for the 'village' then stood at a place south of the present railway station, called, in Gaelic, *Bealaidh-Achadh*, or the Broom field, quite a mile from Cnoc na Rath. The prophecy has to some extent been fulfilled, for the last erection at Beauly – the new public school – is within a few yards of the Cnoc; and the increasing enterprise of the inhabitants is rapidly aiding, and, indeed, will soon secure, the absolute realization of the Seer's prediction.

At the time of the prediction, Beauly stood south of the railway station at least a mile from Cnoc na Rath. At the turn of the century a new school was built there. Today it is part of the town.

In connection with this prophecy we think that we have discovered a Celtic origin for the term Beauly. It is generally supposed to have been derived from the French word *Beaulieu*. The village being originally at *Bealaidh-Achadh*, and so called when the present Beauly was nowhere, what can be more natural than the supposition that the inhabitants carried the original name of their original village along with them, and now present us with the Gaelic *Bealaidh*, anglified into Beauly. This is not such a fine theory as the French one, but it is more likely to be the true one, and is more satisfactory to the student of Gaelic topography.

We have several versions of the prophecy regarding the carrying away of the stone bridge across the River Ness, which stood near the place where the present suspension bridge stands. Mr Macintyre supplies the following, and Mr Maclennan's version is very much the same: – 'He foretold that the Ness bridge would be swept away by a great flood, while crowded with people, and while a man riding a white horse and a woman *enciente* were crossing it. Either the prophet's second sight failed him on the occasion, or tradition has not preserved the correct version of the prediction, for it is well known that no human being was carried away by the bridge when it was swept away by the extraordinary flood of 1849.'

As a matter of fact, there was no man riding a white horse on the bridge at the time, but a man – Matthew Campbell – and a woman were crossing it, the arches tumbling one by one at their heels as they flew across; but they managed to reach the western shore in safety, just as the last arch was crumbling under their feet. Campbell, who was behind, coming up to the woman, caught her in his arms, and with a desperate bound cleared the crumbling structure.

It seems that this prophecy might refer to an earlier occasion. In 1663, according to old records of Inverness, the wooden bridge was extensively repaired with eighty trees brought over from Norway. Two years later it collapsed with two hundred men, women and children upon it. The cause was a beam inadvertently sawn through by a joiner doing repairs. Although four of the townsmen broke legs and thighs, and several more were slightly injured, no one was killed. In 1670, it was decided to replace the wooden bridge with a stone one.

The Seer also foretold that before the latter prediction was fulfilled 'people shall pick gooseberries from a bush growing on the stone ledge of one of the arches'. There are many now living who remember this gooseberry bush, and who have seen it in bloom and blossom, and with fruit upon it. It grew on the south side of the bridge, on the third or fourth pier, and near the iron grating which supplied a dismal light to the dungeon which in those days was the Inverness prison. Maclean, 'A Nonagenarian', writing forty years ago, says nothing of the bush, but, while writing of the predicted fall of the bridge, states, with regard to it, that 'an old tradition or prophecy is, that many lives will be lost at its fall, and that this shall take place when there are seven females on the bridge, in a state poetically described as that "in which ladies wish to be who love their lords".' This was written, as will be seen by comparing dates, several years before the bridge was carried away in 1849, showing unmistakably that the prophecy was not concocted after the event.

A further prophecy regarding the bridges of Inverness has been brought to light by Mr Ian C. Young of Ipswich, who writes as follows:

'The suspension bridge which stood at the foot of Bridge Street in Inverness was condemned in 1937, and it was agreed that a temporary traffic bridge be placed alongside to relieve the strain on the old bridge and also as an alternative crossing while the old bridge was being dismantled. A letter printed in the *Inverness Courier* pointed out that the Seer had said that when it would be possible to cross the River Ness dryshod in five places, a frightful disaster would strike the entire world. If the temporary bridge was put into use *before* the suspension bridge was closed to foot traffic, the forecast would be proved, for there would then be five bridges. The construction went ahead, the temporary bridge was opened for traffic during the last few days of August 1939, and Hitler marched his troops into Poland on 1 September. There are few people who were living in Inverness during those months who do not believe that World War II was forecast by the Seer.'

Further predictions regarding the Inverness bridges have caught the attention of the press over recent years as follows:

'When there are nine (or seven) bridges over the Ness, Inverness will be consumed in fire and flood.'

In 1978 when the Highland Regional Council was considering the erection of another bridge over the River Ness, an anxious rate-payer rang one of the committee members to warn of the prophecy. The story was recorded in the *People's Journal*, 23 September 1978. Counting the three bridges that link the Ness Islands the proposed new construction would have been the ninth bridge. (Or seventh if you count the Ness Bridges as one.) Building started on the new Friars Bridge in 1984. The others are as follows: Railway Bridge, Greig Street Footbridge, Black Bridge, Ness Bridge, Infirmary Footbridge and three small bridges linking the islands.

In 1992 the Railway Bridge was swept away in a flood and in 1995 the Eastgate Hotel was destroyed in a massive fire. Both these happenings are thought to have been a partial fulfilment of the prediction.

'The natural arch, or *Clach tholl*, near Storehead in Assynt, will fall with a crash so loud as to cause the laird of Leadmore's cattle, twenty miles away, to break their tethers.' This was fulfilled in 1841, Leadmore's cattle having one day strayed from home to within a few hundred yards of the arch, when it fell with such a crash as to send them home in a frantic fright, tearing everything before them. Hugh Miller refers to this prediction, as also to several others, in the work already alluded to – *Scenes and Legends of the North of Scotland*, pp 161, 162, 163.

This source is quoted in full on pages 32, 33.

About sixteen years ago, there lived in the village of Baile Mhuilinn, in the West of Sutherlandshire, an old woman of about 95 years of age, known as Baraball n'ic Coinnich (Annabella Mackenzie). From her position, history, and various personal peculiarities, it was universally believed in the district that she was no other than the Baraball n'ic Coinnich of whom the Brahan Seer predicted that she would die of the measles. She had, however, arrived at such an advanced age, without any appearance or likelihood of her ever having that disease, that the prophet was rapidly losing credit in the district. About this time the measles had just gone the round of the place, and had made considerable havoc among old and young; but when the district was, so to speak, convalescent, the measles paid Baraball a visit, and actually carried her away, when within a few years of five score, leaving no doubt whatever in the mind of the people that she had died as foretold centuries before by the famous Coinneach Odhar.

The Seer, one day, pointing to the now celebrated Strathpeffer mineral wells, said: – 'Uninviting and disagreeable as it now is, with its thick crusted surface and unpleasant smell, the day will come when it shall be under lock and key, and crowds of pleasure and health seekers shall be seen thronging its portals, in their eagerness to get a draught of its waters.'

The medical history of Strathpeffer Spa extends back for nearly two hundred years, when the local inhabitants first discovered the healing properties of the waters. The springs produced natural hot water from both iron and sulphur wells, and at one time the visitor would be offered a glass of pure clear water from one tap, then the guide would top it up with clear water from a second tap. As soon as the waters were mixed, however, the glass contained a black fluid which stank vilely. This natural result of mixing iron and sulphur gave rise inevitably to the legend that the devil washed in Strathpeffer! Among the early records of the Spa there is a request from Colin

Avoch. The Seer foresaw the day when every fisherman here would own his cottage

Foulis Castle, seat of Clan Munro

Balnagown Castle. Though greatly altered over the years, this was where Catherine Ross, Lady Foulis, was born in the 16th century

Brahan Castle (from an old water colour). Demolished shortly after the Second World War

Isabella, wife of Kenneth, third Earl of Seaforth
by David Scougal

Kenneth, third Earl of Seaforth, by an unknown Dutch artist. These portraits hang in Fortrose Town Hall

Francis Humberston Mackenzie, 'The last Lord Seaforth'.
A miniature by an unknown artist

Fortrose Cathedral. Burial site of the Seaforth Mackenzies

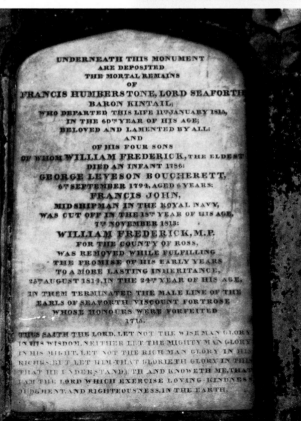

UNDERNEATH THIS MONUMENT
ARE DEPOSITED
THE MORTAL REMAINS
OF
FRANCIS HUMBERSTONE, LORD SEAFORTH
BARON KINTAIL;
WHO DEPARTED THIS LIFE 11ᵀʰ JANUARY 1815,
IN THE 60ᵀʰ YEAR OF HIS AGE;
BELOVED AND LAMENTED BY ALL:
AND
OF HIS FOUR SONS
OF WHOM WILLIAM FREDERICK, THE ELDEST
DIED AN INFANT 1786:
GEORGE LEVESON BOUCHERETT,
6ᵀʰ SEPTEMBER 1794, AGED 6 YEARS:
FRANCIS JOHN,
MIDSHIPMAN IN THE ROYAL NAVY,
WAS CUT OFF IN THE 18ᵀʰ YEAR OF HIS AGE,
7ᵀʰ NOVEMBER 1813:
WILLIAM FREDERICK, M.P.
FOR THE COUNTY OF ROSS,
WAS REMOVED WHILE FULFILLING
THE PROMISE OF HIS EARLY YEARS
TO A MORE LASTING INHERITANCE,
25ᵀʰ AUGUST 1814, IN THE 24ᵀʰ YEAR OF HIS AGE.

IN THEM TERMINATED THE MALE LINE OF THE
EARLS OF SEAFORTH VISCOUNT FORTROSE
WHOSE HONOURS WERE FORFEITED
1715.

THUS SAITH THE LORD, LET NOT THE WISE MAN GLORY
IN HIS WISDOM, NEITHER LET THE MIGHTY MAN GLORY
IN HIS MIGHT, LET NOT THE RICH MAN GLORY IN HIS
RICHES: BUT LET HIM THAT GLORIETH GLORY IN THIS
THAT HE UNDERSTANDETH AND KNOWETH ME, THAT
I AM THE LORD WHICH EXERCISE LOVING-KINDNESS
JUDGMENT, AND RIGHTEOUSNESS, IN THE EARTH.

Memorial tablet in Fortrose Cathedral to 'the last Lord Seaforth' and his four fair sons

The Hood Memorial. This monument was erected by Lady Hood Mackenzie in memory of her sister, the Hon Caroline Mackenzie, who was accidentally killed when thrown from a pony carriage driven by her sister in 1823, thus fulfilling the final part of the great Seaforth prediction that the 'white coifed lassie from the east' should kill her sister

THIS STONE COMMEMORATES
THE LEGEND OF COINNEACH ODHAR
BETTER KNOWN AS THE
BRAHAN SEER
MANY OF HIS PROPHECIES WERE
FULFILLED AND TRADITION HOLDS
THAT HIS UNTIMELY DEATH BY
BURNING IN TAR FOLLOWED HIS FINAL
PROPHECY OF THE DOOM OF THE
HOUSE OF SEAFORTH

Commemorative Stone cast by the boys of Fortrose Academy in 1969 at Chanonry Point, Fortrose, allegedly the site of the Seer's burning

Mackenzie, factor of the Earl of Cromartie's estate, dated 1777, for a suitable building to enclose the springs. He wrote: 'The minister of the parish caused to be erected a kind of building about this well to preserve it from being abused by cattle', and goes on to state that for £6 a proper building could be put up. In 1778, it was resolved to 'give as much as was needed' to preserve the wells from harm. It was left, however, to Dr Thomas Morrison of Elsick, Aberdeenshire, to bring wider prominence to the virtues of the waters. He wrote to the proprietors of the County of Ross in 1818 expressing 'his gratitude for health restored from an illness which for fifteen years had baffled the leading medical practitioners in Britain', and urging them to give every possible assistance to the establishment of Strathpeffer as a Spa. Through his strong personality and enthusiasm, Strathpeffer became widely known and the Spa grew steadily in size and renown. It is still a favourite holiday resort, though the pumprooms have been closed for some years.

Regarding the 'land-grasping Urquharts of Cromarty' he predicted 'that, extensive though their possessions in the Black Isle now are, the day will come – and it is close at hand – when they will not own twenty acres in the district.' This, like many of his other predictions, literally came to pass, although nothing could then have been more unlikely; for, at the time, the Urquharts possessed the estates of Kinbeachie, Braelangwell, Newhall and Monteagle, but at this moment their only possession in the Black Isle is a small piece of Braelangwell.

A contemporary of the first three Earls of Seaforth, Sir Thomas Urquhart was born in 1613 in Cromarty Castle, a literary genius who wrote a treatise on arithmetic and invented a universal language. He was also a Loyalist, taken prisoner at the Battle of Worcester in 1651, where he was said to have lost a hundred of his manuscripts on the battlefield. During his confinement in the Tower of London he translated the first three books of Rabelais in such a style that his translations have been called better than the original. To convince Cromwell of his own importance and that of his clan, this delightful eccentric wrote *The True Pedigree of the Urquhart Family*, in which he traced his ancestry back to Adam and Eve, and named Prince Achaia of Greece in 2159 BC as the 'father of all that carry the name of Urquhart', himself being 143rd in descent. Cromwell was not impressed and is said to have remarked that it was high time that a family who had enjoyed the good things of life for so long was extinguished. Fortunately Sir Thomas escaped to Holland, where he died, so it is said, in a fit of laughter on hearing of the Restoration of the Monarchy. During his time the Urquhart family not only possessed vast tracts of land, but had been hereditary Sheriffs of Cromarty since the days of Robert the Bruce. Walter Urquhart is named as Sheriff in both writs calling for the arrest of the historical Coinneach Odhar in 1577/1578.

True to the prediction, by the second half of the eighteenth century practically all their possessions had gone. Their great castle at Cromarty, last inhabited by an old woman and a young girl, was razed to the ground and a mansion house built close to the site by a new owner. The present Chief of Urquhart is an American, and all he owns in the Black Isle is the ruin of Castlecraig, another ancient Urquhart stronghold, perched on the south shore of the Cromarty Firth.

That 'the day will come when fire and water shall run in streams through all the streets and lanes of Inverness', was a prediction, the fulfilment of which was quite incomprehensible, until the introduction of gas and water through pipes into every corner of the town.

Inverness was one of the first towns in Scotland to have its own Gas Works, opened in 1826 by the Inverness Gas and Water Company, with gas street lighting.

'The day will come when long strings of carriages without horses shall run between Dingwall and Inverness, and more wonderful still, between Dingwall and the Isle of Skye.' It is hardly necessary to point out that this refers to the railway carriages now running in those districts.

The ceremony of cutting the first sod of the railway from Inverness to Dingwall, known as the 'Inverness and Ross-shire Line', took place on 19 September 1860, and it was opened two years later. It was extended to Strome in 1879 and to Kyle in 1897, and is known now as the Highland Line.

That 'a bald black girl will be born at the back of the Church of Gairloch' (*Beirear nighean mhaol dubh air cùl Eaglais Ghearrloch*), has been fulfilled. During one of the usual large gatherings at the Sacramental Communion a well-known young woman was taken in labour, and before she could be removed she gave birth to the *nighean mhaol dubh*, whose descendants are well known and pointed out in the district to this day as the fulfilment of Coinneach's prophecy.

That 'a white cow will give birth to a calf in the garden behind Gairloch House', has taken place within the memory of people still living; that, in Fowerdale, 'a black hornless cow (*Bo mhaol dubh*) will give birth to a calf with two heads', happened within our own recollection. These predictions were well known to people before they came to pass.

The following are evidently fragments regarding the Lovat Estates. He said:

Thig fear tagair bho dheas,
Mar eun bho phreas.
Fasaidh e mar luibh,
'S sgaoilidh e mar shiol,
'S cuiridh e teine ri Ardrois.

(A claimant will come from the South
Like a bird from a bush;
He will grow like an herb;
He will spread like seed,
And set fire to Ardross.)

'*Mhac Shimidh ball-dubh, a dh'fhagus an oigreachd gun an t-oighre dligheach.*' (Mac Shimidh (Lovat), the black-spotted who will leave the Estate without the rightful heir.) '*An Sisealach claon ruadh, a dh'fhagus an oighreachd gun an t-oighre dligheach.*'

(Chisholm, the squint-eyed, who will leave the estate without the rightful heir.) '*An tighearna storach a dh'fhagus oighreachd Ghearr-loch gun an t-oighre dligheach.*' (The buck-toothed laird who will leave the estate of Gairloch without the rightful heir), are also fragments.

We do not know whether there has been any Lovat or Chisholm with the peculiar personal characteristics mentioned by the Seer, and shall be glad to receive information on the point, as well as a fuller and more particular version of the prophecy. We are aware, however, that Sir Hector Mackenzie of Gairloch was buck-toothed, and that he was always known among his tenants in the west, as *An tighearna storach*. We heard old people maintaining that Coinneach was correct even in this instance, and that his prediction has actually been fulfilled; but, at present, we abstain from going into that part of this family history which would throw light on the subject. A gentleman is trying to assert rights to the Lovat estates at the present moment.

Not all the Frasers in Scotland belong to the Highland branch, as the family originally came from Normandy and was to settle in many parts of the country. Founder of the Lovat line was Hugh Fraser, mentioned as Lord of 'Loveth' in 1367. What was to become known as Fraser Country comprised some twenty-eight miles of the low-lying fertile land at the head of the Beauly Firth, and also some Highland territory in Stratherrick, Strathglass and Strathfarrar. In 1544 the clan was seriously reduced by one of the bloodiest fights in Highland history, and thereafter followed a succession of minorities and altercations as to who should be chief.

By the time of the Civil War, however, when the clan had recovered, there were twenty-six cadet branches living in the clan country, compared with five a century before. The clan was divided again after the death in 1696 of Hugh, Lord Lovat, who left a daughter, Amelia, but no sons. Lord Saltoun, chief of all the Frasers, planned a marriage for her with his own son, but the heir male, Simon of Beaufort, would not have it. Saltoun was seized and threatened with death unless he promised to go no further with his match-making, and Amelia was married to a Mackenzie who took the name of Fraser of Fraserdale, while Simon was forced to escape to France. Simon then returned to help oust the Jacobites from Inverness and, as a reward, was pardoned and Fraserdale attainted. So Simon got the title, but promptly lost it and his life by his double-dealing in and before 1745.

The succession passed to the Strichen line in 1815, and later too the title was restored. The present Macshimidh is the 25th clan chief and 18th Lord Lovat.

Since the above was in type, we came across the following in Anderson's *History of the Family of Fraser*, p 114: 'Hugh, son of the 10th Lord Lovat, was born on the 28th September, 1666. From a large black spot on his upper lip he was familiarly called Mac Shimidh Ball-dubh, i.e., black-spotted Simpson or Lovat. Three chieftains were distinguished at this time by similar deformities – (1) Mac Coinnich Glùn-dubh, i.e., black-kneed Mackenzie; (2) Macintoshich Claon, i.e., squint-eyed Mackintosh; (3) Sisealach Cam, crooked or one-eyed Chisholm.'

Before proceeding to give such of the prophecies regarding the family of Seaforth as have been so literally fulfilled in the later annals of that once great and powerful house – the history of the family being so intimately interwoven with, and being itself really the fulfilment of the Seer's predictions – it may interest the reader to have a cursory glance at it from the earliest period in which the family appears in history.

The following fulfilled predictions all ascribed to the Brahan Seer have been heard over the past twenty years.

'The day will come when a war will end at Loch Eriboll.'

Quoted in the sixth edition of the Blue Guides book, this literally came to pass when the German U-Boats gathered to surrender in the deep inlet of Loch Eriboll in Caithness in May 1945.

'When a flock of geese are seen in the streets of Golspie, the sea will flood the town.'

This was heard in Rogart in 1986. It is thought to have been fulfilled many years ago.

'There will be a time when iron will fly in the sky and a stuttering king will be on the throne with a Scottish Queen.' This was quoted in

Dalibrog in 1989 and obviously referred to the coming of aeroplanes and the reign of George VI and Queen Elizabeth, now the Queen-Mother.

With regard to royalty, the Inverness archivist came across a letter from a Beauly ironmonger, John Paterson, to the factor of the Knoydart estate dated June 25 1902 in which he writes:

'How unfortunate to the nation is the illness of the King (Edward VII) and what a disappointment to many. We can only hope and pray that his life will be spared. According to the prophecies of the Brahan Seer, Coinneach Odhar, he said 'A King would reign over Britain, but would never be crowned'. So watch the prophecy . . .'

At the time the prediction was obviously thought to refer to Edward VII who recovered from an appendectomy and was duly crowned. However the prophecy may have referred to King Edward VIII who abdicated in 1936 and was never crowned.

A variation of that prophecy was known in Skye in 1918 which said, 'The day will acome when a king will be born but never crowned. Be sure there will be troublesome times ahead.'

Three years after the abdication of Edward VIII, the Second World War was declared.

'When there are three queens in Scotland summer will be turned to winter, and winter to summer.'

Queen Mary, Queen Elizabeth the Queen Mother and Queen Elizabeth II were all alive for nine months in 1952. This prediction was well known in the Outer Isles and quoted in the *Bulletin* of 26 March 1953, when apart from a storm in January the weather had been exceptionally mild.

A local prophecy about a house near the Muir of Ord states that 'As long as the beech trees stand at Arcan there will be no son born in that house'.

The laird who repeated the prediction in 1989 has three daughters and his predecessor had no sons.

A prediction from Lochalsh contributed by Mrs M. Mackay stated that 'The time will come when houses on wheels will pass over the Aird Ferry.'

It was said to have been realised with the building of the Dornie Bridge in the Lochalsh district over which caravans continually cross in the tourist season.

'When the people of Dornie can walk dry-shod to Kintail, a battle will follow.'

This too was fulfilled when Dornie Bridge was completed. The battle is thought to have been with some government department.

A much older prediction states that 'When the iron horse is seen at Strome Ferry, Dornie will run with blood.'

This foresaw the coming of the Highland railway. When the line reached Strome Ferry, a bad harvest forced the crofters to 'bleed' their cattle for sustenance.

A clutch of predictions refer to the Uists and Benbecula. 'When a black horseshoe is seen, a frightful disaster will over take the world.' This was recorded by Francis Thompson in *The Supernatural Highlands* and was thought to foresee the Second World War before which the North Uist ring road was left unfinished on its northern side, thus presenting a bird's eye view which looked like a black horseshoe.

'The day will come when North Uist will be encircled with steel.' This foresaw the advent of electricity pylons and cables.

'When a road runs up Eaval the second clearance will come and the island will be populated by green men and grey geese.'

'The day will come when the islands will be full of bent grass and big grey geese.'

The 'big grey geese' is a good description of aircraft while the green men aptly describe soldiers from the Royal Artillery Range Hebrides stationed in Benbecula.

Finally another Mackenzie prediction quoted by Duncan Macpherson in *Gateway to Skye* (1946) stated as follows: 'The last of the Seaforths is doomed to marry a crofter'.

This was Mrs Anstruther Mackay a well-kent figure who usually dressed in a heavy woollen jersey and hob-nailed boots as she worked her husband's croft near Kyle in the first half of the twentieth century.

Sketch of the Family of Seaforth

The most popularly-received theory regarding the Mackenzies is that they are descended from an Irishman of the name of Colinas Fitzgerald, son of the Earl of Kildare or Desmond, who distinguished himself by his bravery at the battle of Largs, in 1263. It is said that his courage and valour were so singularly distinguished that King Alexander III took him under his special protection, and granted him a charter of the lands of Kintail, in Wester Ross, bearing date from Kincardine, 9 January 1263.

According to the fragmentary 'Record of Icolmkill', upon which the claim of the Irish origin of the clan is founded, a personage, described as *'Peregrinus et Hibernus nobilis ex familia Geraldinorum'* – that is 'a noble stranger and Hibernian, of the family of the Geraldines' – being driven from Ireland with a considerable number of his followers was, about 1261, very graciously received by the King, and afterwards remained at his court. Having given powerful aid to the Scots at the Battle of Largs, two years afterwards he was rewarded by a grant of the lands of Kintail, which were erected into a free barony by royal charter, dated as above mentioned. Mr Skene, however, says that no such document as this Icolmkill Fragment was ever known to exist, as nobody has ever seen it; and as for Alexander's charter, he declares (*Highlanders*, vol ii, p 235) that it 'bears the most palpable marks of having been a forgery of a later date, and one by no means happy in the execution'. Besides, the words *'Colino Hiberno'* contained in it do not prove this Colin to have been an Irishman, as Hiberni was at that period a common appellation for the Gael of Scotland. Burke, in the *Peerage*, has adopted the Irish origin of the clan, and the chiefs themselves seem to have adopted this theory, without having made any particular inquiry as to whether it was well founded or not. The Mackenzie chiefs were thus not exempt from the almost universal, but most unpatriotic, fondness exhibited by many other Highland chiefs for a foreign origin. In examining the traditions of our country, we are forcibly struck with this peculiarity of taste. Highlanders despising a Caledonian source trace their ancestors from Ireland, Norway, Sweden, or Normandy. The progenitors of the Mackenzies can be traced with greater certainty, and with no less claim to antiquity, from a native ancestor, Gillean (Cailean) Og, or Colin the Younger, a son of Cailean na h'Airde, ancestor of the Earls of Ross; and, from the MS of 1450, their Gaelic descent may now be considered beyond dispute.*

Until the forfeiture of the Lords of the Isles, the Mackenzies always held their lands from the Earls of Ross, and followed their banner in the field, but after the forfeiture of that great and powerful earldom, the Mackenzies rapidly rose on the ruins of the Macdonalds to the great power, extent of territorial possession, and almost regal magnificence for which they were afterwards distinguished among the other great clans of the north. They, in the reign of James I, acquired a very powerful influence in the Highlands, and became independent of any superior but the Crown. Mackenzie and his followers were, in fact, about the most potent chief and clan in the whole Highlands.

Kenneth, son of Angus, is supposed to have commenced his rule in Kintail about 1278, and was succeeded by his son, John, in 1304, who was in his turn succeeded by his son, Kenneth. John, Kenneth's son, was called Iain MacChoinnich, John MacKenneth, or John son of Kenneth, hence the family name Mackenny or Mackenzie. The name Kenneth in course of time became softened down to Kenny or Kenzie. It is well known that, not so very long

* See Nos XXVI and XXVII of the *Celtic Magazine*, Vol III, in which this question is discussed at length.

ago, ʒ in this and all other names continued to be of the same value as the letter *y*, just as we still find it in Menzies, MacFadzean, and many others. There seems to be no doubt whatever that this is the real origin of the Mackenzies, and of their name.

Murchadh, or Murdo, son of Kenneth, it is said, received a charter of the lands of Kintail from David II.

In 1463, Alexander Mackenzie of Kintail obtained the lands of Strathgarve, and other possessions, from John, Earl of Ross. They afterwards strenuously and successfully opposed every attempt made by the Macdonalds to obtain possession of the forfeited earldon. Alexander was succeeded by his son, Kenneth, who married Lady Margaret Macdonald, daughter of the forfeited Earl John, Lord of the Isles; but through some cause,* Mackenzie divorced the lady, and sent her home in a most ignominious and degrading manner. She had only one eye, and Kintail sent her home riding a one-eyed steed, accompanied by a one-eyed servant, followed by a one-eyed dog. All the circumstances exasperated the lady's family to such an extent as to make them ever after the mortal and sworn enemies of the Mackenzies.

Kenneth Og, his son by the divorced wife, became chief in 1493. Two years afterwards, he and Farquhar Mackintosh were imprisoned by James V in Edinburgh Castle. In 1497, however, they both made their escape, but were, on their way to the Highlands, seized, in a most treacherous manner, at Torwood, by the laird of Buchanan. Kenneth Og made a stout resistance, but he was ultimately slain, and Buchanan sent his head as a present to the King.

Leaving no issue, Kenneth was succeeded by his brother John, whose mother, Agnes Fraser, his father's second wife, was a daughter of Lovat. He had several other sons, from whom have sprung other branches of the Mackenzies. As John was very young, his uncle, Hector Roy (Eachainn Ruadh) Mackenzie, progenitor of the house of Gairloch, assumed command of the clan and the guardianship of the young chief. Gregory informs us

---

* For full details of this act, which afterwards proved the cause of such strife and bloodshed, see Mackenzie's *History of the Clan Mackenzie.*

that 'under his rule the Clan Kenzie became involved in feuds with the Munroes and other clans; and Hector Roy himself became obnoxious to the Government as a disturber of the public peace. His intentions towards the young chief of Kintail were considered very dubious, and the apprehensions of the latter and his friends having been roused, Hector was compelled by law to yield up the estate and the command of the tribe to the proper heir.'* John, the lawful heir, on obtaining possession, at the call of James IV, marched at the head of his clan to the fatal field of Flodden, where he was made prisoner by the English, but afterwards escaped.

On King James V's expedition to the Western Isles in 1540, John joined him at Kintail, and accompanied him throughout his whole journey. He fought with his clan at the battle of Pinkie in 1547, and died in 1561, when he was succeeded by his son, Kenneth, who had two sons by a daughter of the Earl of Athole – Colin and Roderick – the latter becoming ancestor of the Mackenzies of Redcastle, Kincraig, Rosend, and several other branches. This Colin, who was the eleventh chief, fought for Queen Mary at the battle of Langside. He was twice married. By his first wife, Barbara Grant of Grant – whose elopement with him will be found described in a poem in the *Highland Ceilidh*, Vol I, pp 215–220, of the *Celtic Magazine* – he had four sons and three daughters, namely – Kenneth, who became his successor; Sir Roderick Mackenzie of Tarbat, ancestor of the Earls of Cromartie; Colin, ancestor of the Mackenzies of Kennock and Pitlundie; and Alexander, ancestor of the Mackenzies of Kilcoy, and other families of the name. By Mary, eldest daughter of Roderick Mackenzie of Davochmaluag, he had a natural son, Alexander, from whom descended the Mackenzies of Applecross, Coul, Delvin, Assynt, and others of note in history.

Kenneth, the eldest son, soon after succeeding his father, was engaged in supporting Torquil Macleod of Lewis, surnamed the 'Conanach', the disinherited son of the Macleod of Lewis, and

---

* *Highlands and Islands of Scotland*, p. III.

who was closely related to himself. Torquil conveyed the barony of Lewis to the Chief of the Mackenzies by formal deed, the latter causing the usurper to the estate, and his followers, to be beheaded in 1597. He afterwards, in the following year, joined Macleod of Harris and Macdonald of Sleat, in opposing James VI's project for the colonization of the Lewis by the well-known adventurers from the 'Kingdom of Fife'.

In 1602, the old and long-standing feud between the Mackenzies and the Macdonalds of Glengarry, concerning their lands in Wester Ross, was renewed with infuriated violence. Ultimately, after great bloodshed and carnage on both sides, an arrangement was arrived at by which Glengarry renounced for ever, in favour of Mackenzie, the Castle of Strome and all his lands in Lochalsh, Lochcarron, and other places in the vicinity, so long the bone of contention between these powerful and ferocious chieftains. In 1607, a Crown charter for these lands was granted to Kenneth, thus materially adding to his previous possessions, power, and influence. 'All the Highlands and Isles, from Ardnamurchan to Strathnaver, were either the Mackenzies' property or under their vassalage, some few excepted,' and all around them were bound to them 'by very strict bonds of friendship'. In this same year Kenneth received, through some influence at Court, a gift, under the Great Seal, of the Island of Lewis, in virtue of, and thus confirming, the resignation of this valuable and extensive property previously made in his favour by Torquil Macleod. A complaint was, however, made to His Majesty by those colonists who survived, and Mackenzie was again forced to resign it. By patent, dated 19 November 1609, he was created a peer of the realm, as Lord Mackenzie of Kintail. Soon after, the colonists gave up all hopes of being able to colonize Lewis, and the remaining adventurers – Sir George Hay and Sir James Spens – were easily prevailed upon to sell their rights to Lord Mackenzie, who at the same time succeeded in securing a grant from the King of that part of the island forfeited by Lord Balmerino, another of the adventurers. He (Lord Mackenzie) now secured a commission of fire and sword against the islanders, soon arrived with a strong force, and speedily reduced them to obedience, with the exception of Neil Macleod and a few of his followers. The struggle between these two continued for a time, but ultimately Mackenzie managed to obtain possession of the whole island, and it remained in the possession of the family until it was sold by the 'Last of the Seaforths'.

This, the first, Lord Mackenzie of Kintail died in 1611. One of his sons, Simon Mackenzie of Lochslin, by his second wife, Isabella, daughter of Sir Alexander Ogilvie of Powrie, was the father of the celebrated Sir George Mackenzie, already referred to. His eldest son, Colin, who succeeded him as second Lord Mackenzie of Kintail, was created first Earl of Seaforth, by patent dated 3 December 1623, to himself and his heirs male. Kenneth, Colin's grandson, and third Earl of Seaforth, distinguished himself by his loyalty to Charles III during the Commonwealth. He supported the cause of the Royalists so long as there was an opportunity of fighting for it in the field, and when forced to submit to the ruling powers, he was committed to prison, where, with much firmness of mind and nobility of soul, he endured a tedious captivity during many years, until he was ultimately released, after the Restoration, by authority of the King. He married a lady descended from a branch of his own family, Isabella Mackenzie, daughter of Sir John Mackenzie of Tarbat, and sister of the first Earl of Cromartie. To her cruel and violent conduct may undoubtedly be traced the remarkable doom which awaited the family of Seaforth, which was predicted in such an extraordinary manner by Coinneach Odhar, fulfilled in its minutest details, and which we are, in the following pages, to place before the reader.

Seaforth's Dream

Before proceeding to relate the Seer's remarkable prediction, and the extraordinary minuteness with which it has been fulfilled, we shall give the particulars of a curious dream by Lord Seaforth, which was a peculiar forecast of the loss of his faculties of speech and hearing during the latter part of his eventful life. It has been supplied by a member of the family,* who shows an unmistakable interest in everything calculated to throw light on the 'prophecies', and who evidently believes them not to be merely an old wife's tale. We give it *verbatim et literatim*: – 'The last Lord Seaforth was born in full possession of all his faculties. When about twelve years of age, scarlet fever broke out in the school at which he was boarding. All the boys who were able to be sent away were returned to their homes at once, and some fifteen or twenty boys who had taken the infection were moved into a large room, and there treated. After a week had passed, some boys naturally became worse than others, and some of them were in great danger. One evening, before dark, the attendant nurse, having left the dormitory for a few minutes, was alarmed by a cry. She instantly returned and found Lord Seaforth in a state of great excitement. After he became calmer, he told the nurse that he had seen, soon after she had left the room, the door opposite to his bed silently open, and a hideous old woman came in. She had a wallet full of

* The late Colonel John Constantine Stanley, son of Lord Stanley of Alderley, who married Susan Mary, eldest daughter of the late Keith William Stewart Mackenzie of Seaforth.

something hanging from her neck in front of her. She paused on entering, then turned to the bed close to the door, and stared steadily at one of the boys lying in it. She then passed to the foot of the next boy's bed, and, after a moment, stealthily moved up to the head, and taking from her wallet a mallet and peg, drove the peg into his forehead. Young Seaforth said he heard the crash of the bones, though the boy never stirred. She then proceeded round the room, looking at some boys longer than at others. When she came to him, his suspense was awful. He felt he could not resist or even cry out, and he never could forget, in years after, that moment's agony, when he saw her hand reaching down for a nail, and feeling his ears. At last, after a look, she slunk off, and slowly completing the circuit of the room, disappeared noiselessly through the same door by which she had entered. Then he felt the spell seemed to be taken off, and uttered the cry which had alarmed the nurse. The latter laughed at the lad's story, and told him to go to sleep. When the doctor came, an hour later, to make his rounds, he observed that the boy was feverish and excited, and asked the nurse afterwards if she knew the cause, whereupon she reported what had occurred. The doctor, struck with the story, returned to the boy's bedside and made him repeat his dream. He took it down in writing at the moment. The following day nothing eventful happened, but in course of time, some got worse, a few indeed died, others suffered but slightly, while some, though they recovered, bore some evil trace and consequence of the fever for the rest of their lives. The doctor, to his horror, found that those whom Lord Seaforth had described as having a peg driven into their foreheads, were those who died from the fever; those whom the old hag passed by recovered, and were none the worse; whereas those she appeared to look at intently, or handled, all suffered afterwards. Lord Seaforth left his bed of sickness almost stone deaf; and, in later years, grieving over the loss of his four sons, absolutely and entirely ceased to speak.'

We shall now relate the circumstances connected with the prophecy, and continue an account of the Seaforth's connection with it to the end of the chapter.

Seaforth's Doom

Kenneth, the third Earl, had occasion to visit Paris on some business after the Restoration of King Charles II, and after having secured his liberty. He left the Countess at Brahan Castle unattended by her lord, and, as she thought, forgotten, while he was enjoying the dissipations and amusements of the French capital, which seemed to have many attractions for him, for he prolonged his stay far beyond his original intention.

Brahan Castle was founded in the fourteenth century and rebuilt entirely during the reign of James VI who gave grants of additional land in the Brahan district, and other portions to the south and west of Dingwall, to Mackenzie of Kintail on his appointment as Commissioner in charge of portions of the royal properties in Ross-shire. Brahan Castle was the scene of stirring activities and romantic episodes in the religious struggles and Jacobite risings. It was for a time occupied by government troops – a garrison 'planted upon Seafort's nose' – and it was here, after the Disarming Act, that the Mackenzie clan laid down their weapons. On the day appointed, over eight hundred clansmen who acknowledged Seaforth as chief filed before General Wade and laid down their arms at Brahan Castle. The heads of families including the Earl of Cromartie and Sir Colin Mackenzie of Coul, entered into an agreement to transfer their loyalty from Prince Charles Edward and the Stuarts to King George and the Hanoverians. The main body of clansmen, their weapons attached to the backs of their Highland ponies, marched in fours up to the steps of the Castle entrance, where Wade and his officers received them. Refreshment was served so that they could drink a loyal toast. In the following year Seaforth received the

King's Pardon. The Castle was demolished soon after the Second World War, and the ground where it once stood is now a great green spread of grass.

Lady Seaforth had become very uneasy concerning his prolonged absence, more especially as she received no letters from him for several months. Her anxiety became too strong for her power of endurance, and led her to have recourse to the services of the local prophet. She accordingly sent messages to Strathpeffer, summoning Coinneach to her presence, to obtain from him, if possible, some tidings of her absent lord. Coinneach, as we have seen, was already celebrated, far and wide, throughout the whole Highlands, for his great powers of divination, and his relations with the invisible world.

Obeying the orders of Lady Seaforth, Kenneth arrived at the Castle, and presented himself to the Countess, who required him to give her information concerning her absent lord. Coinneach asked where Seaforth was supposed to be, and said that he thought he would be able to find him if he was still alive. He applied the divination stone to his eyes, and laughed loudly, saying to the Countess, 'Fear not for your lord, he is safe and sound, well and hearty, merry and happy.' Being now satisfied that her husband's life was safe, she wished Kenneth to describe his appearance; to tell where he was now engaged, and all his surroundings. 'Be satisfied,' he said, 'ask no questions, let it suffice you to know that your lord is well and merry.' 'But,' demanded the lady, 'where is he? with whom is he? and is he making any preparations for coming home?' 'Your lord,' replied the Seer, 'is in a magnificent room, in very fine company, and far too agreeably employed at present to think of leaving Paris.' The Countess, finding that her lord was well and happy, began to fret that she had no share in his happiness and amusements, and to feel even the pangs of jealousy and wounded pride. She thought there was something in the Seer's looks and expression which seemed to justify such feelings. He spoke sneeringly and maliciously of her husband's occupations, as much as to say, that he could tell a disagreeable tale if he would.

The lady tried entreaties, bribes and threats to induce Coinneach to give a true account of her husband, as he had seen him, to tell who was with him, and all about him. Kenneth pulled himself together, and proceeded to say – 'As you will know that which will make you unhappy, I must tell you the truth. My lord seems to have little thought of you, or of his children, or of his Highland home. I saw him in a gay-gilded room, grandly decked out in velvets, with silks and cloth of gold, and on his knees before a fair lady, his arm round her waist, and her hand pressed to his lips.' At this unexpected and painful disclosure, the rage of the lady knew no bounds. It was natural and well merited, but its object was a mistake. All the anger which ought to have been directed against her husband, and which should have been concentrated in her breast, to be poured out upon him after his return, was spent upon poor Coinneach Odhar. She felt the more keenly, that the disclosures of her husband's infidelity had not been made to herself in private, but in the presence of the principal retainers of her house, so that the Earl's moral character was blasted, and her own charms slighted, before the whole clan; and her husband's desertion of her for a French lady was certain to become the public scandal of all the North of Scotland. She formed a sudden resolution with equal presence of mind and cruelty. She determined to discredit the revelations of the Seer, and to denounce him as a vile slanderer of her husband's character. She trusted that the signal vengeance she was about to inflict upon him as a liar and defamer would impress the minds, not only of her own clan, but of all the inhabitants of the counties of Ross and Inverness, with a sense of her thorough disbelief in the scandalous story, to which she nevertheless secretly attached full credit. Turning to the Seer, she said, 'You have spoken evil of dignities, you have defamed a mighty chief in the midst of his vassals, you have abused my hospitality and outraged my feelings, you have sullied the good name of my lord in the halls of his ancestors, and you shall suffer the most signal vengeance I can inflict – you shall suffer the death.'

Coinneach was filled with astonishment and dismay at this fatal result of his art. He had expected far other rewards from his art of divination. However, he could not at first believe the rage of the Countess to be serious; at all events, he expected that it would soon evaporate, and that, in the course of a few hours, he would be allowed to depart in peace. He even so far understood her feelings that he thought she was making a parade of anger in order to discredit the report of her lord's shame before the clan; and he expected that when this object was served, he might at length be dismissed without personal injury. But the decision of the Countess was no less violently conceived than it was promptly executed. The doom of Coinneach was sealed. No time was to be allowed for remorseful compunction. No preparation was permitted to the wretched man. No opportunity was given for intercession in his favour. The miserable Seer was led out for immediate execution.

Such a stretch of feudal oppression, at a time so little remote as the reign of Charles II, may appear strange. A castle may be pointed out, however, viz, Menzies Castle, much less remote from the seat of authority, and the Courts of Law, than Brahan, where, half a century later, an odious vassal was starved to death by order of the wife of the chief, the sister of the great and patriotic Duke of Argyll!

This presumably refers to Christian Campbell, Lady Menzies, wife of Chief Sir Alexander the Menzies, second Baronet, who was daughter of Lord Neil Campbell, second son of the Marquis of Argyll, 1676–1730.

When Coinneach found that no mercy was to be expected either from the vindictive lady or her subservient vassals, he resigned himself to his fate. He drew forth his white stone, so long the instrument of his supernatural intelligence, and once more applying it to his eyes, said – 'I see into the far future, and I read the doom of the race of my oppressor. The long-descended line of Seaforth will, ere many generations have passed, end in extinction and sorrow. I see a chief, the last of his house, both deaf and dumb. He will be the father of four fair sons, all of whom he will follow to the tomb. He will live careworn and die mourning, knowing

that the honours of his line are to be extinguished for ever, and
that no future chief of the Mackenzies shall bear rule at Brahan or
in Kintail. After lamenting over the last and most promising of his
sons, he himself shall sink into the grave, and the remnant of his
possessions shall be inherited by a white-coifed (or white-hooded)
lassie from the East, and she is to kill her sister. And as a sign by
which it may be known that these things are coming to pass,
there shall be four great lairds in the days of the last deaf and dumb
Seaforth – Gairloch, Chisholm, Grant and Raasay – of whom one
shall be buck-toothed, another hare-lipped, another half-witted,
and the fourth a stammerer. Chiefs distinguished by these personal marks shall be the allies and neighbours of the last Seaforth;
and when he looks around him and sees them, he may know that
his sons are doomed to death, that his broad lands shall pass away
to the stranger, and that his race shall come to an end.'

When the seer had ended this prediction, he threw his white
stone into a small loch, and declared that whoever should find that
stone would be similarly gifted. Then submitting to his fate, he was
at once executed, and this wild and fearful doom ended his strange
and uncanny life.

Sir Bernard Burke, to whose *Vicissitudes of Families* we are
mainly indebted for this part of the Prophecies, says: – With
regard to the four Highland lairds, who were to be buck-toothed,
hare-lipped, half-witted and a stammerer – Mackenzie, Baronet of
Gairloch; Chisholm of Chisholm; Grant, Baronet of Grant; and
Macleod of Raasay – I am uncertain which was which. Suffice it
to say, that the four lairds were marked by the above-mentioned
distinguishing personal peculiarities, and all four were the contemporaries of the last of the Seaforths.

We believe Sir Hector Mackenzie of Gairloch was the buck-
toothed laird (*an Tighearna Storach*); the Chisholm, the hare-
lipped; Grant, the half-witted; and Raasay, the stammerer, all of
whom were contemporaries of the last Lord Seaforth.

In the Wardlaw Manuscript, the Rev James Fraser writes:
'Another prediction of some alteration upon the famelies when

black-kneed Seaforth, black-spotted Lord Lovat, squint-eyed Mackintosh and a Chisholm blind of an eye; and these four are just now contemporary: and though much stress should not be laid upon such prophesies, yet they ought not to be vilified or contemnd; and seeing these things were observed before they came, we can do no less than remark then when they fall out, as now they doe. And I remember to heare a very old man, Eneas M'kdonell in Craigscorry, relate this prediction to Sir James Fraser, tutor of Lovat, anno 1648; and as I heard the observe then with my eares, so I now see it with my eyes. God Almighty turn all to the best!'

With regard to the black-spotted Lovat, Fraser gives a full acount of his birth:

'My Lord Lovat . . . got a sudden call from south. . . . He left his lady big with child, in continuall feare. It pleased God she was safely brought to bed of a sone, September 28, being Michaelmas eve; and the child being tender by his mother's former indisposition he was presently christened Hugh. . . . The midwife, Janet Fraser, daughter of Donald, son of Robbie, an honest widow in Finask, told myselfe instantly, "Take well about your young cheefe, the Master of Lovat, for his mother will never bear another." He was born with a large black spot uppon his upper right lip. When Kathrin M'kenzie, Mistress of Kingily, one of the godmothers, got him in her lap, and spying the mark, she said to the midwife "Berwom E Berwom E (*Beir uam e, beir uam e*, Take him from me) take him, away with him, he will do no good", and alas future events proved it true. His mother, my Lady Lovat, whither by apprehension or naturall contingent hysterick fit, was like to passe; but beside the skillfull midwife, Doctor George Mackenzie was domestick, and Jean Turnbull, her own maid, had good preactices of such maladies, which made us fear the lesse. Now is our old prediction confirmed of four considerably chiftens in the North born with signall marks, of which the Master of Lovat is one. . . . All four are so, and whither for good or evil to raise or ruin their famelies, they are signally marked and remarked.'

Elizabeth Grant of Rothiemurchus, in her *Memoirs of a Highland Lady*, writes of the year 1815:

'My last year's friend, the new member for Ross-shire, Mr Mackenzie of Applecross, was at this Meeting, more agreeable than ever, but looking extremely ill. . . . He was a plain man, and he had a buck tooth to which someone had called attention, and it was soon the only topic spoken of, for an old prophecy ran that whenever a mad Lovat, a childless ——, and an Applecross with a buck tooth met, there would be an end of Seaforth. The buck tooth all could see, the mad Lovat was equally conspicuous, and though Mrs —— had two handsome sons born after several years of childless wedlock, nobody ever thought of fathering them on her husband. In the beginning of this year Seaforth, the Chief of the Mackenzies, boasted of two promising sons; both were gone, died within a few months of each other. The Chieftainship went to another branch, but the lands and the old Castle of Brahan would descend after Lord Seaforth's death to his daughter Lady Hood – an end of *Cabarfeidh*. This made everyone melancholy, and the deaths of course kept many away from the Meeting.'

The Seer's Death

Mr Macintyre supplies the following account of the Seaforth prophecy and the Seer's death, as related at this day, in the Black Isle:

Coinneach's supernatural power was at length the cause which led to his untimely and cruel death. At a time when there was a convivial gathering in Brahan Castle, a large concourse of local aristocratic guests was present. As the youthful portion were amusing themselves in the beautiful grounds or park surrounding the castle, and displaying their noble forms and features as they thought to full advantage, a party remarked in Coinneach Odhar's hearing, that such a gathering of gentlemen's children could rarely be seen. The Seer answered with a sneer, 'that he saw more in the company of the children of footmen and grooms than of the children of gentlemen', (*Is mo th'ann do chlann ghillean-buird agus do chlann ghillean-stabuil no th'ann do chlann dhaoin' uaisle*), a remark which soon came to the ears of Lady Seaforth and the other ladies present, who were so much offended and provoked at this base insinuation as to the paternity of the Brahan guests, that they determined at once to have condign punishment on the once respected Seer. He was forthwith ordered to be seized; and, after eluding the search of his infuriated pursuers for some time, was at last apprehended. Seeing he had no way of escape, he once more applied the magic stone to his eye, and uttered the well-known prophetic curse [already given] against the Brahan family, and then threw the stone into a cow's footmark, which was full of water, declaring that a child would be born with two navels, or as some say, with four thumbs and six toes, who would in course of time discover it inside a pike, and who then would be gifted with Coinneach's prophetic power. As it was the purpose of his pursuers to obtain possession of this wonderful stone, as well as of the prophet's person, search was eagerly made for it in the muddy waters in the footprint, when, lo! it was found that more water was copiously oozing from the boggy ground around, and rapidly forming a considerably lake, that effectually concealed the much-coveted stone. The waters steadily increased, and the result, as the story goes, was the formation of Loch Ussie (Oozie). The poor prophet was then taken to Chanonry Point, where the stern arm of ecclesiastical authority, with unrelenting severity, burnt him to death in a tar-barrel for witchcraft.

It is currently reported that a person answering to the foregoing description was actually born in the neighbourhood of Conon, near Loch Ussie, and is still living. Of this I have been credibly informed by a person who saw him several times at the Muir of Ord markets.

We see from the public prints, our correspondent humorously continues, that the Magistrates and Police Commissioners of Dingwall contemplate to bring a supply of water for *Baile-'Chail* from Loch Ussie. Might we humbly suggest with such a view in prospect, as some comfort to the burdened ratepayers, that there may be, to say the least, a probability in the course of such an undertaking of recovering the mystic stone, so long compelled to hide its prophetic light in the depths of Loch Ussie, and so present the world with the novel sight of having not only an individual gifted with second sight, but also a Corporation; and, further, what would be a greater terror to evil-doers, a magistracy capable, in the widest sense of the word, of discerning between right and wrong, good and evil, and thus compelling the lieges in the surrounding towns and villages to exclaim involuntarily – *O si sic omnes!* They might go the length even of lending it out, and giving you the use of it occasionally in Inverness.

When Coinneach Odhar was being led to the stake, fast bound

with cords, Lady Seaforth exultingly declared that, having had so much unhallowed intercourse with the unseen world, he would never go to Heaven. But the Seer, looking round upon her with an eye from which his impending fate had not banished the ray of joyful hope of rest in a future state, gravely answered – '*I* will go to Heaven, but *you* never shall; and this will be a sign whereby you can determine whether my condition after death is one of everlasting happiness or of eternal misery; a raven and a dove, swiftly flying in opposite directions will meet, and for a second hover over my ashes, on which they will instantly alight. If the raven be foremost, you have spoken truly; but if the dove, then my hope is well-founded.'

This prophecy was also attributed to Michael Scot or Scott, the thirteenth-century philosopher who may possibly have been born in Balwearie, Fife, but was more probably a Borderer. He was a remarkable scholar who studied Arabic, astrology and alchemy at Oxford, travelled to Paris, Padua and Toledo to study theology, chemistry and medicine. He served the Emperor Frederick II as royal astrologer and physician, and published among other works a collection of his predictions. In Scotland he was known as Auld Michael, a notorious necromancer who wrote a mighty book of spells which included a recipe for flight, and which was buried with him. His death was said to have been due to supping a broth of breme, a sow in heat, but in Italy legend has it that he was killed by a falling stone.

And, accordingly, tradition relates that after the cruel sentence of his hard-hearted enemies had been executed upon the Brahan Seer, and his ashes lay scattered among the smouldering embers of the faggot, his last prophecy was most literally fulfilled; for those messengers, emblematically denoting – the one sorrow, the other joy – came speeding to the fatal spot, when the dove, with characteristic flight, closely followed by the raven, darted downwards and was first to alight on the dust of the departed Coinneach Odhar; thus completely disproving the positive and uncharitable assertion of the proud and vindictive Lady of Brahan, to the wonder and consternation of all the beholders.

Mr Maclennan describes the cause of Coinneach's doom in almost identical terms; the only difference being, that while the former has the young ladies amusing themselves on the green outside, the latter describes them having a grand dance in the great hall of the Castle. The following is his account of the prophet's end:

In terms of her expressed resolution, Lady Seaforth, some days after this magnificent entertainment, caused the Seer to be seized, bound hand and foot, and carried forthwith to the Ness of Chanonry, where, despite his pitiful looks and lamentable cries, he was inhumanly thrown, head foremost, into a barrel of burning tar, the inside of which was thickly studded with sharp and long spikes driven in from the outside. On the very day upon which Coinneach was sent away from the castle to meet his cruel fate, Lord Seaforth arrived, and was immediately informed of his Lady's resolution, and that Coinneach was already well on his way to the Chanonry, where he was to be burned that very day, under clerical supervision and approval. My lord, knowing well the vindictive and cruel nature of his Countess, believed the story to be only too true. He waited neither for food nor refreshment; called neither for groom nor for servant, but hastened immediately to the stable, saddled his favourite steed with his own hands, for lairds were not so proud in those days, and set off at full speed, hoping to reach Chanonry Point before the diabolical intention of her ladyship and her religious (!) advisers should be carried into effect. Never before nor since did Seaforth ride so furiously as he did on that day. He was soon at Fortrose, when he observe a dense smoke rising higher and higher from the promontory below. He felt his whole frame giving way, and a cold sweat came over his body, for he felt that the foul deed was, or was about to be, perpetrated. He pulled himself together, however, and with fresh energy and re-doubled vigour, spurred his steed, which had already been driven almost beyond its powers of endurance, to reach the fatal spot to save the Seer's life. Within a few paces of where the smoke was rising the poor brute could endure the strain no longer; it fell down under him and died on the spot. Still determined, if possible, to arrive in time, he rushed forward on foot, crying out at the height of his voice to those congregated at the spot, to save their victim. It was, however, too late, for whether Seaforth's cries were heard or not, the victim of his lady's rage and vindictive nature had been thrown into the burning barrel a few moments before his intended deliverer had reached the fatal spot.

The time when this happened is not so very remote as to lead us to suppose that tradition could so grossly blunder as to record such a horrible and barbarous murder by a lady so widely and well known as Lady Seaforth was, had it not taken place.

It is too much to suppose that if the Seer had been allowed to die a peaceful and natural death, that such a story as this would have ever originated, be carried down and believed in from generation to generation, and be so well authenticated in many quarters as it now is. It may be stated that a large stone slab, now covered under the sand, lies a few yards east from the road leading from Fortrose to Fort George Ferry, and about 250 yards north-west from the lighthouse, which is still pointed out as marking the spot where this inhuman tragedy was consummated, under the eyes and with the full approval of the highest dignitaries of the Church.

A stone commemorating the legend of the Brahan Seer and his burning at Chanonry Point was erected by Fortrose Town Council and Academy near the Lighthouse in 1969. Half-way between the Lighthouse and the Golf Clubhouse, on a ridge in the rough, there stands another much older stone. This is said to mark the spot where the last witch was burned, but it is not known who this was, or when. An ancient title deed to one of the original crofts near the neck of the Ness recorded the site of 'Coinneach Odhar's stone', but this has been removed in the recent development of the area.

Some ten years ago the local lighthouse-keeper was approached by a woman in distress who asked if she could bury something in front of the Seer's commemorative stone. She believed her family was still under the influence of Coinneach Odhar's curse and hoped to alleviate it. The keeper told her to do as she pleased, and next day he noticed that a neat rectangle of turf had been cut out and replaced. Such is the power of the Brahan Seer in the Highlands to this day.

The Fulfilment of the Seaforth Prophecy

Having thus disposed of the Seer himself, we next proceed to give in detail the fulfilment of the prophecies regarding the family of his cruel murderer. And we regret to say that the family of Seaforth will, in this connection, fall to be disposed of finally and for ever, and in the manner which Coinneach had unquestionably predicted. As already remarked, in due time the Earl returned to his home, after the fascinations of Paris had paled, and when he felt disposed to exchange frivolous or vicious enjoyment abroad for the exercise of despotic authority in the society of a jealous Countess at home. He was gathered to his fathers in 1678, and was succeeded by his eldest son, the fourth Earl. It is not our purpose to relate here the vicissitudes of the family which are unconnected with the curse of Coinneach Odhar, further than by giving a brief outline, though they are sufficiently remarkable to supply a strange chapter of domestic history.

The fourth Earl married a daughter of the illustrious family of Herbert, Marquis of Powis, and he himself was created a Marquis by the abdicated King of St Germains, while his wife's brother was created a Duke. His son, the fifth Earl, having engaged in the rebellion of 1715, forfeited his estate and titles to the Crown; but in 1726 his lands were restored to him, and he, and his son after him, lived in wealth and honour as great Highland chiefs. The latter, who was by courtesy styled Lord Fortrose, represented his native county of Ross in several Parliaments about the middle of last century. In 1766, the honours of the peerage were restored to his son, who was created Viscount Fortrose, and in 1771, Earl of Seaforth; but those titles, which were Irish, did not last long, and became extinct at his death in 1781.* None of these vicissitudes were foretold in the Seer's prophecy; and, in spite of them all, the family continued to prosper. That ruin which the unsuccessful rising in 1715 had brought upon many other great houses, was retrieved in the case of Seaforth, by the exercise of sovereign favour; and restored possessions and renewed honours preserved the grandeur of the race. But on the death of the last Earl, his second cousin, descended from a younger son of the third Earl and his vindictive Countess, inherited the family estates and the chiefdom of the Mackenzies, which he held for two short years, but never actually enjoyed, being slain at sea by the Mahrattas, at Gheriah, in the south of India, in 1783, after a gallant resistance. He was succeeded by his brother, in whom, as the last of his race, the Seer's prophecy was accomplished.

Francis Humberston Mackenzie was a very remarkable man. He was born in 1754, and although deaf, and latterly dumb, he was, by the force of his natural abilities and the favour of fortune, able to fill an important position in the world.

Francis Humberston Mackenzie was in fact born in 1755 and inherited the clan in 1794.

It would have been already observed that the 'Last of the Seaforths was born in full possession of all his faculties, and that he only became deaf from the effects of a severe attack of scarlet fever, while a boy in school, which we have previously noticed in connection with his remarkable dream. He continued to speak a little, and it was only towards the close of his life, and particularly during the last two years, that he was unable to articulate – or perhaps, unwilling to make the attempt, on finding himself the last male of his line. He may be said to have, prior to this, fairly recovered the use of speech, for he was able to converse pretty distinctly; but he was so totally deaf, that all communcations were

* Mr Mackenzie is mistaken, the Earl died in 1783. [E.S.]

made to him by signs or in writing. Yet he raised a regiment at the beginning of the great European war; he was created a British peer in 1797, as Baron Seaforth of Kintail; in 1800 he went out to Barbados as Governor, and afterwards to Demerara and Berbice; and in 1808 he was made a Lieutenant-General. These were singular incidents in the life of a deaf and dumb man. He married a very amiable and excellent woman, Mary Proby, the daughter of a dignitary of the Church, and niece of the first Lord Carysfort, by whom he had a fine family of four sons and six daughters. When he considered his own position – deaf, and formerly dumb; when he saw his four sons, three of them rising to man's estate; and when he looked around him, and observed the peculiar marks set upon the persons of the four contemporary great Highland lairds, all in strict accordance with Coinneach's prophecy – he must have felt ill at ease, unless he was able, with the incredulous indifference of a man of the world, to spurn the idea from him as an old wife's superstition.

However, fatal conviction was forced upon him, and on all those who remembered the family tradition, by the lamentable events which filled his house with mourning. One after another his three promising sons (the fourth died young) were cut off by death. The last, who was the most distinguished of them all, for the finest qualities both of head and heart, was stricken by a sore and lingering disease, and had gone, with a part of the family, for his health, to the south of England. Lord Seaforth remained in the north, at Brahan Castle. A daily bulletin was sent to him from the sick chamber of his beloved son. One morning, the accounts being rather more favourable, the household began to rejoice, and a friend in the neighbourhood, who was visiting the chief, came down after breakfast full of the good news, and gladly imparted it to the old family piper, whom he met in front of the Castle. The aged retainer shook his head and sighed – 'Na, na,' said he, 'he'll never recover. It's decreed that Seaforth must outlive all his four sons.' This he said in allusion to the Seer's prophecy; thus his words were understood by the family; and thus members of the family have again and again repeated the strange tale. The words of the old piper proved too true. A few more posts brought to Seaforth the tidings of the death of the last of his four sons.

At length, on 11 January 1815, Lord Seaforth died, the last of his race. His modern title became extinct. The chiefdom of the Mackenzies, divested of its rank and honour, passed away to a very remote collateral, who succeeded to no portion of the property, and the great Seaforth estates were inherited by a white-hooded lassie from the East. Lord Seaforth's eldest surviving daughter, the Honourable Mary Frederica Elizabeth Mackenzie, had married, in 1804, Admiral Sir Samuel Hood, Bart, KB, who was Admiral of the West India station while Seaforth himself was Governor in those islands. Sir Samuel afterwards had the chief command in the Indian seas, whither his lady accompanied him, and spent several years with him in different parts of the East Indies. He died while holding that high command, very nearly at the same time as Lord Seaforth, so that his youthful wife was a recent widow at the time, and returned home from India in her widow's weeds, to take possession of her paternal inheritance. She was thus literally a white-coifed or white-hooded lassie (that is, a young woman in widow's weeds, and a Hood by name) from the East. After some years of widowhood, Lady Hood Mackenzie married a second time, Mr Stewart, a grandson of the sixth Earl of Galloway, who assumed the name of Mackenzie, and established himself on his lady's extensive estates in the North. Thus, the possessions of Seaforth may be truly said to have passed from the male line of the ancient house of Mackenzie. And still more strikingly was this fulfilled, as regarded a large portion of these estates, when Mr and Mrs Stewart Mackenzie sold the great Island of Lewis to Sir James Matheson.

After many years of happiness and prosperity, a frightful accident threw the family into mourning. Mrs Stewart Mackenzie was one day driving her younger sister, the Hon Caroline Mackenzie, in a pony carriage, among the woods in the vicinity of Brahan Castle. Suddenly, the ponies took fright, and started off at a furious pace. Mrs Stewart Mackenzie was quite unable to check them, and both she and her sister were thrown out of the carriage much bruised and hurt. She happily soon recovered from the accident, but the injury which her sister sustained proved fatal, and, after lingering for some time in a hopeless state, she died, to the inexpressible grief of all the members of her family. As Mrs Stewart Mackenzie was driving the carriage at the time of the accident, she may be said to have been the innocent cause of her sister's death, and thus to have fulfilled the last portion of Coinnearch's prophecy which has yet been accomplished.

A monument commemorating this sad accident may be seen on the A835 road between Maryburgh and Contin. The Latin inscription reads as follows.

'*Hic fato ut fertur praedicto abrepta est Francis Baron de Seaforth filia Carolina Mackenzie cujus soror eusdem pericli particeps domus suae redintegrandae spes ultima super fuit. MDCCCXXIII*' (At this point, according to the prophecy uttered, Caroline Mackenzie daughter of Francis, Baron Seaforth, was snatched from life; her sister who shared the same hazard was the last surviving hope of restoration of his house. 1823)

The inscription is important for it shows that the prediction was known before the accident.

The monument, smothered in undergrowth since the recent upgrading of the road which runs through the Brahan estate, is badly in need of massive restoration.

Thus we have seen that the last chief of Seaforth was deaf and dumb; that he had four sons; that he survived them all; that the four great Highland lairds who were his contemporaries were all distinguished by the peculiar personal marks the Seer predicted; that his estates were inherited by a white-coifed or white-hooded lassie from the East; that his great possessions passed into the hands of other races; and that his eldest daughter and heiress was so unfortunate as to be the innocent cause of her sister's death. In this very remarkable instance of family fate, the prophecy was not found out after the events occurred; it had been current for generations in the Highlands, and its tardy fulfilment was marked curiously and anxiously by an entire clan and a whole county.

Seaforth was respected and beloved far and near, and strangers, as well as friends and clansmen, mourned along with him the sorrows of his later years. The gradual development of the doom was watched with sympathy and grief, and the fate of Seaforth has been, during the last half-century of his life, regarded as one of the most curious instances of that second sight for which the inhabitants of the Highlands of Scotland have been so long celebrated. Mr Stewart Mackenzie, the accomplished husband of the heiress of Seaforth, after being for many years a distinguished member of the House of Commons and a Privy Councillor, held several high appointments in the Colonial Dominions of the British Crown. He was successively Governor of Ceylon and Lord High Commissioner of the Ionian Islands, and died, universally beloved and lamented, in the year 1843.

Lockhart in his *Life of Scott*, in reference to the Seaforth prediction, says: 'Mr Morrit can testify thus far – that he heard the prophecy quoted in the Highlands at a time when Lord Seaforth had two sons alive, and in good health, and that it certainly was not made after the event'; and he goes on to tell us that Scott and Sir Humphrey Davy were most certainly convinced of its truth, as also many others who had watched the latter days of Seaforth in the light of those wonderful predictions.

The late Duncan Davisdon of Tulloch, Lord-Lieutenant of the County of Ross, on reading our Second edition, wrote to the author, under date of 21 May 1878, as follows: 'Many of these prophecies I heard of *upwards of 70 years ago, and when many of them were not fulfilled*, such as the late Lord Seaforth surviving his sons, and Mrs Stewart-Mackenzie's accident, near Brahan, by which Miss Caroline Mackenzie was killed.' Tulloch was, he said, during the latter years of Lord Seaforth, a regular visitor at Brahan Castle, and often heard the predictions referred to among members of the family. The letter is in our possession, and it was published, during Tulloch's life, and by his special permission, in Mackenzie's *History of the Mackenzies*, p 267.

An attempt was recently made to sell the remaining possessions of the family, but fortunately, for the present, this attempt has

been defeated by the interposition of the Marchioness of Tweed-
dale and Mrs Colonel Stanley, daughters of the present nominal
possessor of the property. At the time a leading article appeared
in the *Edinburgh Daily Review* giving an outline of the family
history of the Seaforths. After describing how the fifth Earl,
with the fidelity characteristic of his house, 'true as the dial to the
sun', embraced the losing side in 'the Fifteen'; fought at the head
of his clan at Sheriffmuir; how in 1719 he, along with the Marquis
of Tullibardine, and the Earl Marischal, made a final attempt to
bring the 'auld Stewarts back again'; how he was dangerously
wounded in an encounter with the Government forces at Glenshiel, and compelled to abandon the vain enterprise; how he was
carried on board a vessel by his clansmen, conveyed to the Western
Isles, and ultimately to France; how he was attainted by Parliament, and his estates forfeited to the Crown; how all the efforts of
the Government failed to penetrate into Kintail, or to collect any
rent from his faithful Macraes, whom the Seaforths had so often
led victorious from many a bloody conflict, from the battle of
Largs down to the Jacobite Rebellions of 1715 and 1719; and how
the rents of that part of the estates were regularly collected and
remitted to their exiled chief in France, with a devotion and faith-
fulness only to be equalled by their own countrymen when their
beloved 'bonnie Prince Charlie' was a wanderer, helpless and
forlorn, at the mercy of his enemies, and with a reward of £30,000
at the disposal of many a poverty-stricken and starving Highlander, who would not betray his lawful Prince for all the gold in
England; the article continues: 'But their (the Seaforth's) downfall came at last, and the failure of the male line of this great
historical family was attended with circumstances as singular as
they were painful. Francis, Lord Seaforth, the last Baron of
Kintail, was, says Sir Walter Scott, "a nobleman of extraordinary
talents, who must have made for himself a lasting reputation, had
not his political exertions been checked by painful natural in-
firmity". Though deaf from his sixteenth year, and inflicted also
with a partial impediment of speech, he was distinguished for his
attainments as well as for his intellectual activity. He took a lively

interest in all questions of art and science, especially in natural history, and displayed at once his liberality and his love of art by his munificence to Sir Thomas Lawrence, in the youthful straits and struggles of that great artist, and by his patronage of other artists. Before his elevation to the peerage, Lord Seaforth represented Ross-shire in Parliament for a number of years, and was afterwards Lord-Lieutenant of the county. During the revolutionary war with France, he raised a splendid regiment of Ross-shire Highlanders (the 78th, the second which had been raised among his clan), of which he was appointed Lieutenant-Colonel Commandant, and he ultimately attained the rank of Lieutenant-General in the Army. He held for six years the office of Governor of Barbados, and, by his firmness and even-handed justice, he succeeded in putting an end to the practice of slave-killing, which at that time was not unfrequent in the Island, and was deemed by the planters a venial offence, to be punished only by a small fine.

'Lord Seaforth was the happy father of three (four) sons and six daughters, all of high promise; and it seemed as if he were destined to raise the illustrious house of which he was the head, to a height of honour and power greater than it had ever yet attained. But the closing years of this nobleman were darkened by calamities of the severest kind. The mismanagement of his estates in the West Indies involved him in inextricable embarrassments, and compelled him to dispose of a part of his Kintail estates – "the giftland" of the family, as it was termed – a step which his tenantry and clansmen in vain endeavoured to avert, by offering to buy in the land for him, that it might not pass from the family. He had previously been bereaved of two of his sons, and about the time that Kintail was sold, his only remaining son, a young man of talent and eloquence, the representative in Parliament of his native county, suddenly died. The broken-hearted father lingered on for a few months, his fine intellect enfeebled by paralysis, and yet, as Sir Walter Scott says, "not so entirely obscured but that he perceived his deprivation as in a glass, darkly". Sometimes he was anxious and fretful because he did not see his son; sometimes he expostulated and complained that his boy had been allowed to

die without his seeing him; and sometimes, in a less clouded state
of intellect, he was sensible of his loss in its full extent. The last
Cabarfeidh followed his son to the grave in January 1815, and
then –

Of the line of Fitzgerald remained not a male,
To bear the proud name of the Chiefs of Kintail.

'The most remarkable circumstance connected with this sorrowful tale, is the undoubted fact that, centuries ago, a Seer of the
Clan Mackenzie, known as Kenneth Oag (Odhar), predicted that
when there should be a deaf and dumb *Cabarfeidh* (Staghead, the
Celtic designation of the chief of the clan, taken from the family
crest), the "gift-land" of their territory (Kintail) would be sold,
and the male line become extinct. This prophecy was well known
in the north long before its fulfilment, and was certainly not made
after the event. "It connected," says Lockhart, "the fall of the
house of Seaforth not only with the appearance of a deaf *Cabarfeidh*, but with the contemporaneous appearance of various physical misfortunes in several other great Highland chiefs, all of which
are said to have actually occurred within the memory of the
generation that has not yet passed away."

'On the death of his lordship, his estates, with all their burdens
and responsibilities, devolved on his eldest daughter, Lady Hood,
whose second husband was James Stewart Mackenzie, a member
of the Galloway family, and whose son has just been prevented
from selling all that remains of the Seaforth estates. "Our friend,
Lady Hood," wrote Sir Walter Scott to Mr Morritt, "will now be
Caberfeidh herself. She has the spirit of a chieftainness in every
drop of her blood, but there are few situations in which the clever-
est women are so apt to be imposed upon as in the management
of landed property, more especially of a Highland estate. I do fear
the accomplishment of the prophecy that, when there should be
a deaf *Caberfeidh*, the house was to fall." ' The writer concludes
thus: 'Scott's apprehensions proved only too well founded. One

section after another of the estates had to be sold. The remaining portion of Kintail, the sunny braes of Ross, the church lands of Chanonry, the barony of Pluscarden, and the Island of Lews – a principality itself – were disposed of one after the other, till now nothing remains of the vast estates of this illustrious house except Brahan Castle, and a mere remnant of their ancient patrimony (and that in the hands of trustees), which the non-resident, nominal owner has just been prevented from alienating. *Sic transit.*'

The 14,000-acre estate of Kintail is now owned by the National Trust for Scotland. The present owner of Brahan, Andrew Matheson, is a relative of the old Seaforth family and manages the Brahan estate.

Leaving these extraordinary prophecies with the reader, to believe, disbelieve, or explain away on any principle or theory which may satisfy his reason, his credulity, or scepticism, we conclude with the following:

Lament for 'The Last of the Seaforths'

BY SIR WALTER SCOTT

In vain the bright course of thy talents to wrong
Fate deadn'd thine ear and imprison'd thy tongue,
For brighter o'er all her obstructions arose
The glow of the genius they could not oppose;
And who, in the land of the Saxon, or Gael,
Might match with Mackenzie, High Chief of Kintail?

Thy sons rose around thee in light and in love,
All a father could hope, all a friend could approve;
What 'vails it the tale of thy sorrows to tell?
In the spring time of youth and of promise they fell!
Of the line of MacKenneth remains not a male,
To bear the proud name of the Chief of Kintail.

And thou, gentle Dame, who must bear, to thy grief,
For thy clan and thy country the cares of a Chief,
Whom brief rolling moons in six changes have left,
Of thy husband and father and brethren bereft;
To thine ear of affection, how sad is the hail
That salutes thee – the heir of the line of Kintail!

Na 'm biodh an t' earball na bu ruighne biodh
mo sgialachd na b' fhaìde.

Conclusion

Who was Coinneach Odhar?

Where the supernatural is concerned, most people tend to believe what they want to believe, and Highlanders are no exception. Thus, research has been tentative in trying to distinguish between the Coinneach Odhar of tradition and the Ceilidh hearth, and the Coinneach Odhar of historical fact.

Probably the first literary reference to him comes in T. Pennant's *A Tour in Scotland*, 1769. When writing of Sutherland he says: 'Every country has had its prophets. . . . and the Highlands their Kenneth Oaur.'

The Bannatyne Manuscript History of the Macleods, circa 1832, in which he was said to predict the downfall of the Macleods, places him as a native of Ness in the Isle of Lewis, born in the sixteenth century.

Hugh Miller, in his *Scenes and Legends of the North of Scotland* written in 1834, has him a field labourer working in the vicinity of Brahan Castle in the mid-seventeenth century; and Alexander Mackenzie, in the *Prophecies of the Brahan Seer*, tells us that he was a native of Baile-na-Cille in the parish of Uig, Lewis, born in the first half of the seventeenth century.

The only historical reference so far known exists in two Commissions of Justice, ordering the Ross-shire authorities to prosecute a certain Keanoch Owir for witchcraft, dated 1577/1578; and this places him firmly back into the sixteenth century.

Coinneach Odhar would have been a magician indeed to have survived the trial of 1578 only to succumb to the flames a century later, and an even greater gap would seem to separate the personalities of sorcerer and Seer. Who then *was* Coinneach Odhar, and where did he come from?

His prophecies, as has been seen, range over the Outer Hebrides, Skye, through Kintail in Wester Ross, over the Conon area and the Black Isle, as far west as Cromarty and north into Sutherland; but the most famous prophecy, and the one on which his reputation largely rests, concerns the Seaforth Mackenzies. According to Alexander Mackenzie, it was Coinneach's skill as a Seer which first attracted the attention of Kenneth, third Earl of Seaforth, who established him at Brahan as a favourite. There he offended the Countess, Isabella, first during a clan gathering when he remarked that he saw more of worth in the company of gillies and stable-hands than of aristocrats; and then, more seriously when, at her insistence, he 'saw' the Earl's unfaithfulness while in Paris on King Charles II's affairs. According to tradition, she had him arrested for witchcraft and burned in a spiked barrel of tar on the Ness at Fortrose, just too late for the Earl to save him. Before he died, he predicted the extinction of the Seaforth line.

What troubled Highland historians, including Alexander Mackenzie himself, was that they could find no factual proof whatsoever for this well-known, oft-repeated tale. In contrast with the sixteenth century, the seventeenth century was a well-documented period in Scottish history, and yet there is no evidence of Coinneach Odhar's existence, let alone his death, in the contemporary writings or documents of the day.

Alexander Brodie of Brodie and his son James, who kept detailed diaries from 1652 to 1685, and who knew and disliked the Seaforths, do not mention the death of Coinneach Odhar which must surely have created some interest in the surrounding neighbourhood, if not horror; nor does the Rev James Fraser, Minister of Kirkhill and author of the Wardlaw Manuscript, which traces the history of the Frasers from 916 to 1674. The minister knew all the contemporary personalities and wrote of them in gossipy detail, but nowhere does he mention Coinneach Odhar, his trial or his death, although he showed great interest in other witchcraft trials of the day. Unfortunately, the Rosemarkie parish records of the time were destroyed in 1737 when the Session Clerk's house was burned down, but there is no mention of him in other ecclesiastical sources, though Presbytery records were kept in great detail.

In spite of the fact, then, that the Seaforth prediction was widely known before the event, by men of such calibre as Sir Walter Scott, Sir Humphrey Davy and the last Lord Seaforth himself, there was no written evidence that Coinneach Odhar was a Mackenzie, that he was born in Lewis in the seventeenth century, that he suffered a witch's death by order of Isabella. No proof, in fact, that there ever was such a man.

Then, in 1925, the historian Dr William M. Mackenzie, discovered among the Scottish Parliamentary Records of the sixteenth century a Commission of Justice from Holyroodhouse, dated 25 October 1577, and issued to Walter Urquhart, Sheriff of Cromarty, and Robert Munro of Foulis, authorizing them to seek out and apprehend six men and twenty-six women charged with the 'diabolical practices of magic, enchantment, murder, homicide and other offences' within the bounds of the Earldom of Ross, the Lordship of Ardmannach (the Black Isle) and other parts of the Sheriffdom of Inverness. Among those to be arrested were Thomas McAnemoir McAllan McHenrik, alias Cassin-donisch; Mariota Neymaine McAlester, alias Loskoir Longert; and Christina Milla, daughter of Robert Milla. The last name is that of Keanoch Ower – Coinneach Odhar as written by a Lowland clerk – who is described as 'the leading or principal enchantress', no doubt due to the same clerk's inability to distinguish between a male and a female Gaelic name.

Some years later a further commission was discovered among the Foulis archives, given here in full.

1577/8 January 23
Commission under the Quarter Seal appointing Lauchlin Mackin-tosche of Dunnachtane, Colin Mackenzie of Kintail, Robert Munro of Foulis, Walter Urquhart, Sheriff of Cromartie, Hugh alias Hugheon Ross of Kilraok, and Alexander Falconar of Halkartoun, or one, two or three of them, conjunctly and severally, justiciaries within the bounds of the Earldoms of Ross and Moray and Lordship of Ardmanach, and other parts within the sheriffdoms of Innernes, Elgin, Forres and Narne, to apprehend, imprison and try Kenneth alias Kennoch Owir, principal or leader in the art of magic, (blank) Neyeane McAllester alias Loskoloukart and Marjory Miller, daughter of Robert Miller, smith in Assint, and all other men and women using and exercising the diabolical, iniquitous and odious crimes of the art of magic, sorcery and incantation within said bounds, who

shall be named by the ministers within the bounds foresaid each for his own parish.

At Halerudehouse.

Seal appended, slightly damaged.

Here was documentary proof at last that Coinneach Odhar existed, if not in the person or century expected. That we know something about him is due to other names on the writ, in particular that of Mariota McAlester, called Loskoir Longert. The habit of nicknaming has always been the norm in the Highlands and Robert Bain, in his *History of the Ancient Province of Ross*, 1899, translates Loskoir Longert as *Loisg na Lotar*, or 'burn the ladle'. The Rev W. Matheson's interpretation, given in his paper to the Gaelic Society, Inverness, 1968 on the historical Coinneach Odhar, is *Losgadh-luchairt* meaning 'burn the castle', which is probably nearer the mark. Thomas alias Cassindonisch, more correctly spelled *Cas-an-donais*, means 'Devil's foot'.

These and others were implicated in one of the most intriguing witchcraft trials in Scottish history, that of Catherine Ross, Lady Munro of Foulis, which took place in 1590. Her indictment is fully reported in Pitcairn's *Criminal Trials of Scotland* and provides some clues to the profession of Coinneach Odhar without mentioning him by name.

Catherine was the daughter of Alexander Ross, ninth Laird of Balnagown in Easter Ross, second wife of Robert Mor Munro, fifteenth Baron of Foulis, and mother of seven children. The indictment against her is long, repetitive and at times contradictory, but the gist of it accuses Catherine of trying to dispose of her stepson, Robert, heir of Foulis, and her sister-in-law, Marion Campbell of Calder, so that her brother George of Balnagown might be free to marry Robert's wife. She was also accused of attempting to dispose of Robert Mor's other sons by his first wife, so that her son George might inherit the clan. In order to achieve her ambition, she was accused of employing local witches and warlocks to cast prehistoric flint arrow-heads, known as elf-arrows, at images of butter and clay, and when this failed of resorting to ratsbane, which allegedly killed a gillie and her nurse and turned Marion Campbell into an invalid for life.

These crimes were said to have taken place in 1577 when commissions were purchased for the arrest of the local witches, several of whom are known to have been caught and taken to the Chanonry on the Black Isle, the ecclesiastical seat of justice for the Diocese of Ross, where they were tried and at least two were burned to death. According to the indictment, Catherine, protesting her innocence, rode to the Chanonry to offer herself for trial as the poor wretches, no doubt under torture, had named her as ringleader and instigator of the crimes. Whether by her own wish or that of her husband, she was hurried off to Caithness where her uncle, the Earl of Caithness, had the King's power of justice, and there she remained for nearly a year until it was safe to return to Foulis, where she lived unmolested until her husband and protector, Robert Mor, died in 1588.

Her stepson, Robert, on his succession to the clan, purchased a commission for her arrest, but he died before it could be executed. He was succeeded by his youngest brother, Hector, who immediately ordered her arrest. She may have been taken to Edinburgh for trial but was more likely to have been tried in Tain. She was acquitted by a packed jury of Munro and Ross dependants after pleading not guilty on all counts.

On the same day, following her trial, Hector took his place in the dock, accused by her of using witchcraft and poison to get rid of her son George, who had died some months previously. He too was acquitted by a jury of dependants, many of whom had already served on Catherine's assize.

Incredibly, Hector was not only clan chief, but a minister of the Reformed Church, Dean of Ross, and an educated man.

Because the Chanonry Cathedral records for this period are missing, thought by some to be lost in the Vatican archives, there is no proof that Coinneach Odhar was ever caught; but if he had been taken and tried, it is reasonable to suppose that as 'principal enchanter' he too would have been convicted and burned for witchcraft on Chanonry Ness.

At first sight it would appear that there could be little to link the Coinneach Odhar who was a warlock with the Brahan Seer of a century later, that there might perhaps have been two Coinneach Odhars; but on closer examination of the few facts available, there is much to connect the sorcerer with the Seer.

For example, both men met misfortune through involvement with strong-minded unpopular women. Lady Isabella was not liked. Although she was the daughter of Sir John Mackenzie of Tarbat, a sister of the first Earl of Cromartie and a first cousin of her husband, the Revd James Fraser wrote in 1660, the year of her wedding, that Lord Seaforth had married 'a kinswoman of his own, a daughter of Lord Tarbuts, after all men's hopes of him, debases himselfe mean spirited to marry below himself, getting neither beauty, parts, portion, relation'. A fairly damning inditement that may have been true on at least two counts. Her father was too impoverished to give her much of a dowry and she was certainly not pretty.

Brodie of Brodie is equally forthright. In his diary for 1676 he writes: . . .

> July 31. My Ladi Seaforth cald; and we being from home, she went to Darnaway.
>
> Aug 1. My Ladi Seaforth went by and cald not; I reveranc the Lord's providence.

Her portrait shows that she was not beautiful in the conventional sense, but lively, intelligent, quick-tempered perhaps, undeniably forceful. She spent most of her married life moving from one impoverished estate to another. Brahan Castle was at that time part derelict, for the Kintail fortune had been squandered in the cause of the Restoration and the estates confiscated during the Commonwealth.

Fraser tells us that in 1667, at the funeral of the Chief of Munro, there were a thousand Rosses on foot, six hundred Munros, but Seaforth was accompanied by a few horses only. 'It is a thing I wonder at that nobleman, that he makes no figure at all at burials,' said Fraser disapprovingly. Seaforth could not afford it.

Both Brodie and Fraser suggest that the Earl was a heavy drinker. In 1671 when Isabella was brought to bed of one of her eight children in Lewis, the Earl sent for the Laird of Raasay to witness the christening. After the sacred ceremony, Raasay – with presumably the Earl's co-operation – indulged in a bout of heavy drinking on the shore and was later drowned with all his attendants. 'Drunkenness did the mischief,' the minister reported.

Brodie writes sanctimoniously in his diary entry for July 5, 1673: 'I heard of the great drinking betwixt the Earl of Seaforth and Aboin. Alac! God dishonoured and not in al ther thoghts.'

Thus Isabella had to be tough, thrifty and no doubt made herself unpopular as a result. After her husband's death in 1676, her life was largely occupied with the troubles of her son, the fourth Earl. When he died in 1701 she wrote of him that 'he was the great joy of my life and support of my age'.

Thereafter she organized the life of her grandson, the fifth Earl, until her death in Edinburgh in 1715. She was buried in the Church of Holyroodhouse, 'at the north side betwixt the fourth and fifth pillars from the west'.

Isabella was a capable self-willed woman, who no doubt did much to save the Seaforth estates from bankruptcy and in so doing made herself disliked; a woman capable certainly of punishing a subordinate who dared to criticize her family; but not necessarily the vindictive monster that legend has made her, nor, I suggest, powerful enough to order the arrest, trial and public execution of a servant and thereafter manage to suppress all written evidence.

Nor was the Coinneach Odhar of her era any saint, though folklore has done its best to beatify him. Alexander Mackenzie describes him as 'very shrewd and clear-headed for one in his menial position; was always ready with a smart answer, and if any attempted to raise the laugh at his expense, seldom or never did he fail to turn it against his tormentors'.

Hugh Miller's description of him is similar; 'It is said that when serving as a field labourer with a wealthy clansman who resided some where near Brahan Castle, he made himself so formidable to the clansman's wife by his shrewd sarcastic humour, that she resolved on destroying him by poison.' Some might go further and say that he had decidedly unpleasant characteristics, well suited to a sorcerer. When he suspected that his dinner had been poisoned, Mackenzie tells us that 'to test the truth of the vision he gave the dinner to his faithful collie. The poor brute writhed and died soon after in the greatest agony.'

Isabella and her Seer were perhaps two of a kind.

Catherine Ross has also been condemned too easily as an evil woman, who not only used witchcraft and poison to gain her ends but who was ultimately responsible for the burning of subordinates whose worst crime lay in obeying her orders.

Catherine's father, Alexander Ross, was a violent undisciplined man who feared neither God, the King nor Parliament, and who was the scourge not only of neighbouring clans but also of his own people. Fearing that his folly would bring about the ruin of the Rosses, fourteen lesser chieftains signed a petition exhorting him to behave lest he 'perish, his house, kyn and friends and tyne the rigges that his fathers wan'. Although he was deposed in favour of his son, George, and imprisoned in Tantallon Castle, he died at Ardmore in 1592, an unrepentant old man with letters of fire and sword issued against him.

Catherine's husband, Robert Mor Munro, could not have been more different. First in line of the Highland chiefs to vote in the Reformation Parliament of 1560, he also entertained and supported Mary, Queen of Scots, on her visit to Inverness in 1562. He was a man of stature both physical and mental, who was Chamberlain of Ross, Keeper of Dingwall Castle and Customar of Inverness-shire. He added greatly to clan lands and prosperity and was held in high regard both by Parliament and his own clan. His first wife, Margaret Ogilvie, by whom he had six children, was a daughter of Baron Findlater, friend of Mary of Guise and widow of Lachlan Mackintosh of Mackintosh.

Some short while after his first wife's death, he married Catherine of Balnagown. He must have known the crimes of which she was accused, for he was one of the justiciaries appointed by the Crown to arrest her alleged accomplices. When they confessed that it was at her instigation that poison had been bought and used, he must have arranged for her retreat to Caithness until the heat had died down, whether for the honour of the clan or because he believed in her innocence, we do not know. But he fetched her home to Foulis some nine months later, where she was to remain in peace until his death. She bore him seven children.

Whether Catherine was seriously involved in witchcraft or whether this is a sorry tale of jealousy between the two families of Robert Mor, we shall probably never know. Certainly the years 1588 to 1590 were bad for the clan. Robert Mor, its pillar and pivot, died in November 1588. A few months later, his son and heir, Robert, died leaving no sons. About this time his second son, Hugh, must also have died, for he is mentioned in a deed a year or so earlier; so it was his third son, Hector, who inherited the clan. In June 1589, Catherine's eldest son, George, died also in mysterious circumstances. So many deaths must have engendered accusations and counter-accusations, resulting in the rekindling of old grievances and culminating in the two trials, which in their turn must have caused a great deal of unpleasantness and infighting among the elders of the clan.

That Catherine, Hector, and probably Catherine's brother, George, were all involved to a certain extent in occult practices, and that because of it others had to pay the ultimate penalty, seems likely. Catherine and her brother were related to Francis, fifth Earl of Bothwell, who in 1591 was himself to stand trial for witchcraft and treason; and some years later George was accused by King James VI of giving him shelter and support during his escape to Caithness.

It is therefore possible that the historical Coinneach Odhar, described as 'principal enchanter', was in fact burned at Chanonry some time in 1578 and that *Catherine Ross*, not Isabella Mackenzie, was the cause of his death.

Seer and sorcerer are also linked – though somewhat tenuously – through the use of poison. The historical Coinneach Odhar had, through association with Catherine Ross, some dealings with poison. The Brahan Seer, according to both Hugh Miller and Alexander Mackenzie, became aware of his power to predict through the use of poison. In Hugh Miller's version, the wife of his employer mixed a preparation of noxious herbs with his food and brought it to him in a pitcher while he was cutting peats. As he was asleep at the time, she left it by his side and returned home. He awoke, found a stone pressing coldly against his heart, looked through it and 'saw' what she had done. In Mackenzie's version, his wife brought him his dinner, left it for him and went home. He felt the stone under his head, looked through it and 'saw' that his food had been polluted, though not intentionally, and thus was saved. Mr Matheson suggests that this might be a case of role reversal; a plot to poison others in the service of a woman, turned in the telling to a plot by a woman to murder himself – another case of legend seeking to whitewash the Seer.

A further link may lie in the Brahan Seer's use of a divining stone.

Stones possessing magical virtues were famous throughout Highland history. St Columba was said to possess one, also St Declan. There was a pebble in Aberfeldy shaped like a human heart which was said to cure cattle disease. In Skye, stones were used to cure cramp. The Frog Stone set in King Frog's head was of immense value, and the *Clach Nathrach*, or Serpent Stone, formed from the sweat of writhing snakes, was famous for its magical properties and is an undoubted relic of Druidism. Throughout the superstitious past, stones in various shapes and forms have been carefully treasured as heirlooms possessing magical power. The historical Coinneach Odhar might well have possessed such a stone in his trade as sorcerer, but no other stone written about or told of in Scottish folklore is associated with the gift of second sight. Andrew Lang, in his Foreword, suggests that the Seer's possession of such a stone turned him into a crystal-gazer rather than a man of vision, for the fact that true second sight is unsought and involuntary would obviate the use of any such aid.

We are told in Hector Munro's indictment that he 'socht responses and consultations' from the witches he employed. In other words, he commanded them to predict the future for him. Possibly the historical Coinneach Odhar was 'a principal in the art of magic' just because he could cultivate the art of prediction in the same way, and for the same sort of reason, as the Witch of Endor herself. It is reasonable to suppose that such a man would have an assortment of magical charms, including a divining stone.

The location of Seer and sorcerer could be another link between the two persons. There is no solid evidence that Coinneach Odhar was born or lived in Lewis, or indeed ever left the region of Easter Ross, though Hugh Miller suggests that he may have visited Sutherland. Mr Matheson has an ingenious theory which shows how many of the tales and prophecies connected with the Seer might have come to originate in Lewis.

When, at the beginning of the seventeenth century, the Mackenzies wrested Lewis from the Macleods, a certain George Mackenzie was tacksman of Baile-na-Cille. His mother was a Munro of Kaitwell in Easter Ross, and therefore closely connected to the Munros of Foulis. She spent her latter years living with her son, and no doubt many of her tales round the hearth centred on the Munro witchcraft trials and on the deeds of the principal enchanter himself. So popular were these tales to become, so vivid to the imagination of the Lewismen, that as time passed it must have seemed as if both stories and characters originated from Baile-na-Cille itself. This would tie up with the fact that Frances Tolmie, the well-known collector of Lewis folk music (1840–1926), though she searched carefully among the old records of the district, was never able to trace anything which suggested that Coinneach Odhar had been born there.

(It would not, however, account for the Coinneach Odhar of the Bannatyne Manuscript, who is said to be a native of Ness in Lewis, a contemporary of Tormad Mcleod, who died in 1585 and who was allegedly buried in Ness, having had little or no connection with East Ross-shire.)

Conclusion: Who Was Coinneach Odhar?

As will be seen in the Commentary, many of the legends and prophecies connected with Coinneach Odhar in Lewis owe their origin to Norse folklore and other seers. Indeed, many of his prophecies could have been made by anyone at any time, and some have been attributed to Thomas the Rhymer and the philosopher, Michael Scot. *The Prophecies of True Thomas*, published in 1615 by Andro Mart of Edinburgh, was sold all over the Highlands and so taken to heart by the people of Inverness that they began to associate him with the fairies of Tomnahurich. The legend relating to the raven and the dove which would alight on the Seer's ashes, was also told of Michael Scot.

Coinneach Odhar allegedly said: 'The day is coming when the jaw-bone of the big sheep will put the plough on the hen roost.'

The Isla Seer prophesied: 'The time is coming when the sheep's tooth will take the coulter out of the ground in Isla.'

Thomas the Rhymer said, 'The teeth of the sheep shall lay the plough on the shelf.'

No man can tell who first uttered these predictions, or how old they are. As Mr Matheson says, 'The name of Coinneach Odhar seems to have acted like a magnet, drawing a host of prophetic utterances to itself.' Canon Macleod of Macleod, who edited the Bannatyne Manuscript in 1927, calls his predictions 'nothing more than prophetic history'.

Finally, in the Gaelic tradition there is no mention at all of the 'Brahan Seer', only of Coinneach Odhar, with the occasional addition of 'Seer'. This style belongs solely to Alexander Mackenzie, who no doubt thought it an imaginative title, which it has proved to be, for his book was a best-seller from the start.

It would appear then that Seer and sorcerer might well be the same man – a professional occultist, a clairvoyant dependent upon his stone, a native of Easter Ross whose wit and power brought him into conflict with a woman of equally strong character, and who was eventually to suffer a witch's death at the Chanonry of Ross; a man of such authority and personality that his name became attached as author to a host of prophecies whose exponents have been long forgotten; a sinister creature who has been whitewashed by folklore, turned from villain to hero through wish-fulfilment of both story-teller and listener.

All this may well be true and yet one question remains. Who uttered the Mackenzie prediction which was so widely known and so vividly detailed by Alexander Mackenzie, and by Robert Bain in his *History of the Ancient Province of Ross*?

Conclusion: Who Was Coinneach Odhar?

It was impossible for the historical Coinneach Odhar to have made the Seaforth prophecies, and for two solid reasons. The Seaforth peerage was not created until 1623, thus Coinneach Odhar could not have found favour with an Earl as yet unborn, nor quarrelled with a Countess who did not exist. Secondly, the title 'Earl of Seaforth' was never used by Gaelic-speaking story-tellers of the time. They continued to refer to their chief as Mac Coinneach, which was the age-old style used to address Mackenzie chiefs. As for the title 'Countess of Seaforth', there is no Gaelic equivalent. It has been assumed, therefore, by some historians that because there was no Gaelic usage of the English title, the stories relating to Coinneach Odhar and the Countess can have no basis in fact, and must be the idea of someone using English, possibly Mackenzie himself, who had a lively imagination when it came to handling the original Gaelic stories.

Yet the prophecy known as the doom of the House of Kintail makes no use of these titles. The first part of it, which deals with the Seaforth Mackenzies, is simple, stark and explicit. Moreover it was so well known before its fulfilment that at the time of the death of the last Seaforth it was recounted in practically every newspaper in the country. Research has shown, however, that there are several versions of that second part of the prophecy which mentions the four great lairds, Gairloch, Chisholm, Grant and Raasay (and their distinguishing disfigurements) who would be living in the day of the last Lord Seaforth. The earliest version of this tale is given in the Wardlaw Manuscript by the Rev James Fraser, who refers to it as 'an old prediction', and says that the four lairds were contemporaries of himself; thus the story was old at the time of Isabella and was attached to a different context.

Pennant writing in 1769 also mentions the four lairds as follows: 'Whenever a Macleane with long hands, a Frazier with a black spot on his face, a Macgregor with the same on his knee and a club-footed Macleod of Rasa should have existed .... oppressors would appear in the country, and the people change their own land for a strange one. These predictions, say the good wives, have been fulfilled, and not a single breach in the oracular effusions of Kenneth Oaur.'

Among the mass of prophecies invented after the occasion, those ascribed to other sources and those which might be clever guesswork or sheer invention, there still remains, in my opinion, sufficient to show that someone 'gifted' in the Highland sense of the word was responsible for the Seaforth prediction, and that he may yet be found somewhere amidst the mass of folklore and legend accumulated by Alexander Mackenzie, Hugh Miller and others.

I venture to suggest then that his name might well have been Kenneth Mackenzie. People of that name claiming to be his descendants were still living in the Inverness area and in Glasgow some thirty years ago and there is no reason to doubt their word.

Most likely he was, as Hugh Miller called him, 'a Ross-shire Highlander' of the seventeenth century who, if he was not born in Lewis, may well have travelled there with the Earl as part of his retinue, for by that time the island was owned by the Mackenzies and it is known that Seaforth spent much of his time there. His 'gift' may have caught the attention of the Earl, who gave him employment and no doubt awarded him special privileges in exchange for his company at large gatherings, where he would be expected to predict for the clan. I see him as a reserved man, puritanical perhaps, preferring the quiet of croft and family life to castle ways, disapproving of the feasting and drinking, reproachful of the behaviour of the clan aristocrats, disliked by the chieftains of the district who were angered by his outspoken tongue, constantly in conflict with the Countess; a man of mystery, a little in awe of his own strange powers.

At last, driven beyond endurance by the nagging Countess, he tells her just what this plain, basically insecure, woman does not want to know – that her husband is enjoying himself too much at the court of King Charles II, which he is known to have visited on at least one occasion. She orders the clansmen to seize him. He retaliates with a prophecy that has all the hallmarks of a curse, and which was probably made in the presence of a large gathering. Thereafter he 'disappears' – whether imprisoned or killed or merely dismissed from the Earl's service to lead, as Hugh Miller describes it, 'an unsettled, unhappy kind of life – wandering from place to place, a prophet only of evil, or of little trifling events', is not known.

Probably he was an amalgam of several of the countless Celtic seers to live in the Gaelic heartland over the centuries whose name has, through the oral tradition of the Gael, come to symbolise the whole of Highland prophetic history.

Because of the dramatic nature of the prophecies and the lack of authentic knowledge about their perpetrator, legend has clothed this shadowy figure in the multi-coloured plaid of the traditional Brahan Seer.

Bibliography

ADAM, FRANK, *The Clans, Septs & Regiments of the Scottish Highlands*, 1908

AYRE-TODD, GEORGE, *Early Scottish Poetry*, 1891

BAIN, ROBERT, *History of the Ancient Province of Ross*, 1899

CAMPBELL, JOHN G., *Witchcraft and Second Sight in the Highlands and Islands of Scotland*, 1902 and 1974

CHAMBERS, R., *Popular Rhymes of Scotland*, 1858

CHAMBERS, ROBERT, *Domestic Annals of Scotland (Vol I)* W. and R. Chambers, 1858

Chronicles of the Frasers, known as the Wardlaw Manuscript, Scottish History Society, 1905

Diaries of the Lairds of Brodie 1652–1685, Spalding Club, 1863

GEIKIE, SIR ARCHIBALD, *The Life of Sir Roderick I. Murchison (2 Vols)*, Gregg International, 1973

GRANT, ELIZABETH, *Memoirs of a Highland Lady 1792–1827*, Murray 1972

GRANT, I. F., *Highland Folk Ways*, Routledge & Kegan Paul, 1961

INSULANUS, THEOPHILUS, *A Treatise on Second Sight*, 1763

KENNEDY, DR JOHN, *The Days of the Fathers in Ross-shire*, 1861

KIRK, ROBERT, *The Secret Common-Wealth* (ed Stewart Sanderson), D. S. Brewer for the Folklore Society, 1976

MACDONALD, MHAIRI A., *Were There Two Brahan Seers?*, Scots Magazine, October 1969

MACKENZIE, ALEXANDER, *Historical Tales and Legends of the Highlands*, 1878

MACKENZIE, ALEXANDER, *History of Clan Mackenzie*, 1879

MACKENZIE, ALEXANDER, *History of Clan Munro*, 1898

MACKENZIE, ALEXANDER, *History of the Frasers of Lovat*, 1896

MACKENZIE, OSGOOD, *A Hundred Years in the Highlands*

MACLEOD OF MACLEOD, REV CANON R. C., *The Macleods of Dunvegan, from the Time of Leod to the End of the Seventeenth Century*, Based on the Bannatyne Manuscript, 1927

MACPHERSON, DUNCAN, *Gateway to Skye*, Aeneas Mackay, 1946

MARTIN, MARTIN, *Description of the Western Isles*, 1705

MATHESON, REV WILLIAM, *The Historical Coinneach Odhar and Some Prophecies Attributed to Him*, Transactions of the Gaelic Society, Vol 46, 1968

MILLER, HUGH, *Scenes and Legends of the North of Scotland*, 1834

MORRISON and MACRAE, *Highland Second Sight*, Dingwall, 1908

PENNANT, T., *A Tour in Scotland*, Warrington, 1769

Pitcairn's Criminal Trials in Scotland, Vol I, Bannatyne Club

Scottish Record Society, containing the Calendar of Writs of Munro of Foulis, 1299–1823

SUTHERLAND, ELIZABETH, *Ravens and Black Rain*, Constable, 1985

SWIRE, OTTA F., *The Highlands and their Legends*, Oliver & Boyd, 1963

The Hub of the Highlands, Inverness Field Club and Paul Harris, 1975

THOMPSON, FRANCIS, *The Supernatural Highlands*, Robert Hale, 1976

TOMES, JOHN, *The Blue Guides Scotland*, Ernest Benn Ltd, 1975

TRANTER, NIGEL, *The Fortified House in Scotland*, Vol 5, Chambers, 1970

Index

Albemarle, Duke of, 62
Alexander III (King), 98
Allt nan Torcan, 51 (*and see* MacAulay)
Anderson: *Guide to the Highlands*, 63
Anderson: *History of the Family of Fraser*, 96
Animism, 14
Ard-nan-Ceann (Benbecula), 53
Argyll family, 81, 109
Armorial bearings, 72 (*and see* Mackenzie)
Arpafeelie, 12, 30
Athole, Earl of, 101
Avoch, 70, 72, 73, 87

Baile-na-Cille, 12, 27, 138
  burial ground, 27–8
Baillies (of Dochfour), 80
Bain family, 53
Bain, Robert, 132, 139
Balconie Castle, 88
Balmerino, Lord, 102
Balnagown, Catherine of, 136
  (*and see* Ross, Catherine)
Balwearie (Fife), 115
Bannatyne, Sir William Macleod, of Kames, 28
Bannatyne MS (History of the Macleods), 28, 129, 138, 139
Beaufort, Simon of, 96
Beaufort (*see* Downie Castle)

Beauly, 69, 79, 88–9
  Loch, 41
  origin of name, 89
Benbecula, 61
Bennet, St., 87
Bennettsfield, 87
Bible, the, 11, 15, 26
Bissett, Sir John, 79
Black Isle, 69, 70, 72, 87, 93, 113
  and cattle sickness, 78–9
Bloody Bay, battle of, 65
Boniface, St., 87
Boswell, James, 14, 65
Bothwell, Francis, (5th Earl of), 136
Brahan Seer:
  birth, 12, 27
  estate worker at Brahan Castle, 13, 31
  divining stone, 13, 23, 28, 29, 30, 31, 33, 34, 87, 107, 109–10, 113, 137
  how powers acquired, 29–34
  death, 108–9, 110, 113–17, 130, 136, 139
  pronounces doom of Seaforths, 109–10, 113–14, 118–27, 140–1
  Stone erected at Chanonry Point, 117
  origins and history, 129–41
  knowledge of poisons, 137
  (*and see* Prophecies)
Brahan Castle, 86, 102, 112, 113, 126
  demolished, 107
  derelict, 134

Breac, John, 81, 82
Breadalbane family, 81
Brodie, Alexander, 47, 130, 133, 134
Bruce, Robert the, 93
Buchanan, Hector Macdonald, 81
Burke, Bernard, 43, 110
Burke's *Peerage*, 99

Caithness, 136
Caithness, Earl of, 133
Caledonian Canal, 35–6, 39
Cameron, Alexander (of Lochmaddy), 27
Campbell, Angus (of Ensay), 82
Campbell, Dr. (of Killinver), 80
Campbell, General, 61
Campbell, Mr. (of Knock in Mull), 80
Carr, General, 47
Carysfort, Lord, 120
Castlecraig, 93
Ceilidh, 11, 12
Celtic Magazine, 12, 19, 40, 58, 99n., 101
Chanonry Cathedral, 133
Charles, Prince (*see* Stuart)
Charles I, 88
Charles II, 106, 109, 141
Charles III, 103
Chisholm, 95–6, 110, 140
Cille-Chriosd battles, 57
Civil War, 96
Clach an Tiompain, 43–4, 45
Clach an t-Seasidh Stone, 41–2, 43
Clach Dubh an Abain, 63
Clach n' Tuindain ('Stone of the Turning'), 46
Clach tholl, 91
Clanranald, Lady, 61
Clergy, and second sight, 26–7
Cloutie Well, 87
Coinneach Odhar (*see* Brahan Seer)
Columba, St., 22, 137
Commonwealth, the, 103, 134
Conon river, 41
Craigie Well, 87

Craiguck Well (see Craigie Well)
Cromartie, Earl of, 92, 101, 103, 106
Cromwell, Oliver, 47, 88, 93
Croy, Fox of, 77, 80
'Crystal gazing', 23
Culloden, battle of, 49, 61, 64, 83
Cumberland, Duke of, 64, 83

Da Radharc, 14
Da Shealladh, 14
David II, 88, 100
Davidson family, 53
Davy, Sir Humphry, 26, 123, 130
Days of the Fathers in Ross-shire, The, (1861), 15
Declan, St., 137
Description of the Western Isles of Scotland, 14
Dingwall, 46, 62
Disarming Act, 29, 106
Disruption, the, 57
Divining Stone (*see* Brahan Seer)
Domhnall Dubh, 41
'Donald of the Isles', 46
Dove, legend of the, 115, 138
Downie Castle, 66
Druids, 13–14, 43, 137
Duncraig Castle, 59–60
Dunskaith, 79
Dunvegan Castle, 64–6, 80, 81
    legends concerning, 81, 82

Eagle Stone, 46
Earlston, 37
Eddydor Castle (*see* Redcastle)
Edinburgh Castle, 100
Edinburgh Daily Review, 123
Edinburgh University (Dept. of Celtic Studies), 16
Elgin, 72
Endor, Witch of, 138
Ercildoune, 37

Fairburn Castle, 83–4
Fairburn Tower prophecies, 43
Fairy Flag, 65

Fairy Hill (Tomnahurich), 38–9
Fairy Tower, 65
Fearchair a Ghunna (Farquhar of
  the Gun), 68–9
  (*and see* Maclennan, Farquhar)
Fearn calamity, 23, 56–7
Fenians (*see* Fingal)
Ferrintosh Church, 55–6
Ferrintosh legend, 23
Ferrintosh sandbanks, 37–8
Fettes, Sir William, 79
Findlater, Baron, 136
Fingal (and Fenian warriors), 38, 44
'Fingal's Well', 45
Fiosaiche (*see* Second sight)
Fitzgerald, Colinas, 98
Fletcher family, 72–3
Flodden, 101
Forbes, Bishop, 56
Forbes, Lord President, 86
Fortrose, 47, 116, 117
  family, 118, 119
Foulis archives, 131
Foulis, Lady Munro of (Catherine
  Ross, q.v.), 132, 133, 135, 136,
  137
Fraser, Rev. James, 110, 130, 133,
  134
Fraser, Sir James (Lovat's tutor),
  111
Frasers, of Lovat, 66, 79, 95, 96, 100
France/French, 66, 106–8
  war with, 124
Frederick II, Emperor, 115
Frog Stone, 137

Gaelic Society of Inverness, 40, 132
Gairloch, Laird of, 140
Gairloch House, 50, 94, 100
  (and *see* Prophecies)
  Baronet Mackenzie of, 110
Galloway, Earl of, 121, 126
Genealogy of the Macraes, 62
George II, 106
Germains, St., King of, 118
Glenelg Stone prediction, 54

Glenshiel, battle of, 123
Gneiss Monolith (St. Clement's
  Church, Dingwall), 46
Grant: Barbara, of Grant, 101
  Baronet of, 110
  Elizabeth (of Rothiemurchus), 111
  Laird of, 140
Guide to the Highlands, 63
Guise, Mary of, 136

Hamilton, Patrick, 56
Hanoverians, 64, 66, 106
Harlaw, battle of, (1411), 46
Hay, Sir George, 102
Hegel, and Second sight, 21
Highland Ceilidh, 101
Highlands and Islands of Scotland,
  101n.
*History and Traditions of the Isle of
  Skye*, 27
*History of the Ancient Province of
  Ross*, 132, 139
History of the Clan Mackenzie,
  100n.
History of the Family of Fraser, 96
History of the Mackenzies, 123
Holmes (Jack) Report, (1970), 89
Holyrood House, Commission of
  Justice records, 131
Hood, Admiral, 121
Hood, Lady, 112, 121, 126
Hundred Years in the Highlands, A.
  50
Huntly, Earl of, 52

Insulanus, Theophilus, 14
Invergordon smelter, 49
Inverness, 12, 38–9
Inverness Advertiser, 39
Inverness Courier, 91
Inverness Gaelic Society, 12
Iron Age, 44–5
Isla Seer, 37, 139

Jacobite Memoirs, 56
James I, 99

James II, 79
James IV, 65, 101
James V, 65, 100, 101
James VI, 47, 65, 102, 106, 136
'Jawbone' prophecy, 85–7 (and see
  'Lewsmen')
Johnson Dr. Samuel, 14, 23, 65
Journal of a Tour in the Hebrides, 14

Kennedy, Dr. John, 15
Kilcoy Castle, 78–9
Kilcoy family history, 78–9
Kintail, 42, 98, 99, 100, 106
  Lord Mackenzie of (1609), 102, 103
  resistance to Government, 124
  estate sold, 125, 126
  fortune lost in Restoration, 134
  doom of, 140
Kirk, Rev. Robert (1699), 14
Kisimul Castle, 83
Knockfarrel, 44–5, 46, 86

Land prices, 79
Lang, Andrew, 12, 13, 21, 137
Largs, battle of, 98, 124
Lawrence, Sir Thomas, 124
Learmont, 37
Leod (son of Olaf the Black), 65
Lewis Clearances, 66
Lewis, Isle of, 12, 52, 138
  gift of to Kenneth Mackenzie, 102
  sold to Sir James Matheson, 121
'Lews, Island of', 40
'Lewsmen', 85–6
Life of Scott (Lockhart), 123, 126
Life of the late Dr Norman Macleod,
  80
Lillingstone, Mr. (Lochalsh Estate), 59
Lochalsh, 59, 66, 102
Lochcarron, 102
Lockhart (*see Life of Scott*)
Lovat family, 66, 95, 96, 100
'Lovat of the Black Spot', 110–11,
  112
Lyon, David and William the, 79

MacAulays, massacre of, 51–2

Macbeth, 47
MacCrimmon School of Pipers, 65
Macdonald, Flora, 61
  of Glengarry, 102
  Lady Margaret, 100
  of Sleat, 102
  Philip, 29
  Rev. Dr., 55
  (*and see* Nunton)
Macdonalds, 52, 61, 100, 102
  of Clanranald, 99, 100
Macdonnells (of Glengarry), 58
Mac-Gille-challum (of Raasay), 60–1
McGregor, Rev. Alexander, MA, 12,
  17, 19
Macintosh, 96
  Farquhar, 100
  Lachlan, 136
Macintyre, Mr. (of Arpafeelie), 12,
  30, 36, 67–8, 113
Mackay, Aeneas, 12
Mackenzie, Sir Alexander, 50
  Maj.-Gen. Sir Alexander, 85
  Alexander (Alexander the Knife), 78
  Alexander (the 'Clach'), 12–13, 17,
    40–1, 129, 130, 137, 139
  of Applecross ('with the buck-
    tooth'), 111–12
  Arabella, 91–2 (death from
    measles)
  Hon. Caroline, 121–2, 123
  Capt. Colin, 86
  Colin, 92
  Rev. Colin, 86
  Sir Colin (of Coul), 106
  Francis Humberston (Baron
    Seaforth; Baron Mackenzie of
    Kintail), 13, 119, 120, 121, 124
  Sir George, 69, 71, 72, 73, 74
    and widow's lawsuit, 73–4
    and Leith Walk apparitions, 74–6
  Sir Hector (of Gairloch), 95
  Hector Roy, 100, 101
  11th Baron of Hilton, 86
  Keith William Stewart (of
    Seaforth), 104n.

Index

Kenneth (*see* Brahan Seer)
Osgood, 50
Stewart, 43
Mrs. Stewart, 121-2
Major Thomas, 86
Dr. William M., 131
Mackenzies: feud with
Macdonalds of Glengarry, 102
lands of the, 101-3
origins of the, 98-100
of Coul, 47
of Fairburn, 83-5
of Kilcoy, 76-8, 101
of Lochalsh, 59
of Rosehaugh, 69, 70, 71
of Seaforth, 47
(*and see* Seaforth)
Maclennan, A. B., 12, 15, 37, 41,
63, 78-9, 87
Farquhar, 68-9
Maclennans (of Kintail), 42
Macleod: Rev. Donald, DD, 80
Donald, 40
Dame Flora, 65-6
Neil, 103
Norman ('the third Norman'), 81-2
Rev. Canon R. C., of Macleod,
28, 139
Tormad, 28, 138
Torquil (of Lewis), 101-2
Macleods: Bannatyne History of the,
28, 29, 129
of Harris, 41, 102
of Lewis, 52
of Raasay, 60-1
of Skye, 65-6
Macmillan (of Kilduick), 42
Macneil, Clan, 83
(of Barra), 82, 83
General, 83
R.L., 83
Macraes (of Kintail), 42, 124
Duncan, 61-2
Rev. John, 62
'Maidens of Macleod', 81, 82
Making of Religion, 22

Mart, Andro, 138
Martin, Martin, 14
Mary, Queen of Scots, 135
Mathesons (of Balmacarra), 59
Alexander, MP, 59
Andrew, 126
Sir James, 121
Rev. William, 16, 40, 132
Memoirs of a Highland Lady, 111
'Men, the', 15
Menzies Castle, 109
Middleton, Earl of, 62
Milburn, 83
Miller, Hugh, 31, 32, 91, 129, 135,
137, 138, 140, 141
Moidart, Loch, 61
Monk, General (later Duke of
Albemarle), 62
Monro, Sir George, 62
Moody and Sankey ('two false
teachers'), 47-8
Mor, Robert (Mor Munro), 132, 133
Moray (de Moravia) family, 88
Morrison, Rev. John (the Petty
Seer), 15, 62, 63
Morrison, Dr. Thomas (of Elsick), 92
Morrisons (of Ness in Lewis), 31
(*and see* Macleods of Harris)
Muir of Ord, 41, 57, 66-9
Muir of Tarradale, 68
Munro Clan, 46, 132, 134, 135, 136,
137
My Schools and Schoolmasters, 32

National Trust for Scotland, 126
Nationalist Party (SNP), 88
Neil of the Nine Hostages (High
King of Ireland), 83
Ness, Brahan Seer's grave at, 29
Ness, Bridge over the, 89-90, 91
Ness, Loch, 36
Nickname habit, 131-2
Nigg Bay, 50, 79
Norse mythology, 28, 29, 65, 138
Norway (*see* Norse)
Nunton House, 61

Og, Kenneth, 100
Ogilvie, Margaret, 136
Ogilvie, Sir Alexander (of Powrie), 103
Oil-rig platforms, 49–50
Ord, Mackenzie of, 58
Ord, Muir of (*see* Muir of Ord)
Ord, Red Laird of, 57
Ormond Castle, 88
  sacked by Cromwell, 88

Petty, Parish of, (evictions), 62–3
Petty Seer, The, 12, 62
Petty Stone, 63–4
Picts, 44–5, 46
Pinkie, battle of, 101
Pitcairn's *Criminal Trials of Scotland*, 132
Portland, Duke of, 68
Powis, Herbert, Marquis of, 118
Proby, Mary, 120
Prophecies of Brahan Seer:
  downfall of Macleods, 29
  roads through Highlands, 32, 36
  persecutions, 33
  corpses' ford over river Oikel, 33
  Finnbhein raven drinking blood, 33
  fox in Castle Downie, 33
  cow calving in Fairburn, 33
  white fox in Sutherland, 33
  wild deer taken at Fortrose Point, 33
  dry rivulet in Wester Ross, 33
  deaf Seaforth, 33 (*and see* Seaforth)
  collapse of Chanonry of Ross, 43, 46–7
  Storehead arch collapse, 33, 91 (*and see Clach tholl*)
  Caledonian Canal, 35–6, 39
  depopulation of Highlands, 36–7
  sheep spread through Highlands, 36–7, 48–9, 139
  Tomnahurich Fairies' Hill, 38–9
  Beauly Loch bursting its banks, 41
  Fairburn Tower tree, 43

  the five spires in Strathpeffer, 44
  Beauly river dries up, 48
  royal sturgeon in Beauly estuary, 48
  emigration, 49
  Gairloch House chimneys, 50
  Raanish murder, 52
  Tulloch murders, 53
  Ard-nan-Ceann battle, 53
  Mackenzies and Lochalsh, 59
  Mathesons and Balmaccara, 59–60
  Raasay and Mac-Gille-Challum, 60–1
  and Clan Ranald, 61
  Petty clearances, 62–3
  Petty Stone, 63–4
  railways, 66–9, 94
  Macleod family, 29, 80–2
  Lady Hill (the Ladyhill), 88
  Beauly, 88–9
  Ness bridges, 89–90
  measles, 91–2 (*and see* Arabella Mackenzie)
  Urquhart family, 92–3
  Inverness 'fire and water', 94
  Gairloch House: the 'bald, black girl' 94
  the white cow, 94
  Fowerdale calf with two heads, 94
  Lovat estates, 95–7
Prophecies of the Brahan Seer, 12, 13, 129
Prophecies of True Thomas, (1615), 138
Psychical Research Society's Proceedings, 22

Raanish murders, 52
Raasay Island, 60
Raasay, Laird of, 134, 140
Raasay, Macleod of, 101
Rabelais (see Urquhart, Sir Thomas)
Railways, 66–9
Ranald, Clan, of the Isles, 61
  (*and see* Clanranald)

Raven: superstitions in Norway and
Highlands, 29
and Brahan Seer's death, 115, 138
Rebellions, 86, 118, 119, 123, 124
'Record of Icolmkill', 98
Redcastle, 79–80
seized by the Mackenzies, 79
Reformation, 47, 56
Reformation Parliament, (1560), 135
Restoration of Monarchy, 93, 106,
134
Robinson, T. I., 78
Rosehaugh (*see* Mackenzies)
Rosemarkie Parish records, 130
Ross, Alexander, of Balnagown, 56,
132, 135
Canonry of, 46
Catherine, Lady Munro of Foulis,
132, 133, 135, 136, 137
Earl of, 100
Euphemia, Countess of Ross, 47
Nicholas, 56
Ross-shire Highlanders (the 78th
Regiment), 124
Ruthven, Lord, 47

Saltoun, Lord, 96
Sankey (*see* Moody)
*Scenes and Legends of the North of
Scotland*, 31, 32, 91, 129
Scot, Michael (Auld Michael), 115,
138
Scot's Magazine (1742), 57
Scott, Sir Walter, 26, 124, 125, 126,
130
Lament for Seaforths, 127
Scottish Highlands, The, 12
Seaforth family, 13, 42–3, 98–103
origins of title, 139–40
and Prince Charles Stuart, 86
prophecy concerning, 42–3, 116–17,
140–1
(*and see* Brahan Seer; Mackenzies)
Seaforth, Lord, dream, 104–5
Governor of Barbados, 124–5
journey to Paris, 106–8

loss of speech and hearing, 22,
104–5, 109, 124, 125
Seaforth, Isabella (Mackenzie), 13,
103, 106–12, 130
and witchcraft, 133, 134, 135
(*and see* Brahan Seer)
Second sight, 13–14, 15, 21, 25, 27
Serpent Stone, 137
Sherriffmuir, battle of, 61, 123
Sheil, Loch, 54
'Sir Tristrem', 37
Skene's *Highlanders*, 98
Skye, Isle of, 13, 14, 61, 80
famine, 65–6
Smith, Rev. F. (of Arpafeelie), 56
Spens, Sir James, 102
Stanley, of Alderley, Lord, 104n.
Stanley, Col. John Constantine, 104n.
Stanley, Mrs, Colonel, 123
Storehead (*see* Clach tholl*)
Stornoway, 87
Strathconon, 68
Strathpeffer Wells, 43–4, 45, 46, 92
Strichen family, 96
Strome, Castle of, 102
Stuart, Prince Charles Edward, 50,
61, 64, 86, 106, 124
Summer in Skye, A, 64
'Superstitions of the Highlanders',
12, 19
Sutherland Press, Golspie, 12

taibhs, 14
Taibhs searachd, 14, 25
taibhsear, 14, 15
Tantallon Castle, 135
Tarbat, Sir John Mackenzie of, 103
Tarbat, Sir Roderick Mackenzie of,
101, 133
Tarbert (Harris), 40
Telfer, Thomas, 36
Thomas the Rhymer, 37, 138
Thompson, Francis, 15
Tioram Castle, 61
Tolmie, Frances, 138
Tomnahurich, 35–9, 69, 138

Torachilty dam, 41
Torr-a-Chuilinn (Kintail) rock, 54
Treatise on the Second Sight, A, 14
*True Pedigree of the Urquhart
  Family, The*, 93
Tullibardine, Marquis of, 123
Tulloch Castle, 46
  Laird of, 53, 123
Tweedale, Marchioness, of 123

Urquhart family (of Cromarty), 93
  Sir Thomas, 93
  (*and see* Cromwell)
Urray, Church of, 55
Ussie, Loch, 12, 44, 45, 114

Vatican archives, 133

Vicissitudes of Families, (Sir Bernard
  Burke), 110

Wade, General, 106
*Walford's County Families of the
  U.K.*, 72
Wallace, William, 88
Wardlaw MS, 110, 130, 140
Wars of Independence (1297), 88
White Friars (Abbacy at Ferne
  Church), 56–7
Witchcraft, 129, 130–1, 132, 136, 138
  (*and see* Ross, Catherine)
Witness, The, 32

Young, Ian C., 90–1